Understanding R&D Productivity

The Technology Policy and Economic Growth Series

Herbert I. Fusfeld and Richard R. Nelson, Editors

Fusfeld/Haklisch INDUSTRIAL PRODUCTIVITY AND INTERNATIONAL TECHNICAL COOPERATION
Fusfeld/Langlois UNDERSTANDING R&D PRODUCTIVITY
Hazewindus THE U.S. MICROELECTRONICS INDUSTRY: Technical Change, Industry Growth, and Social Impact
Nelson GOVERNMENT AND TECHNICAL PROGRESS: A Cross-Industry Analysis

Pergamon Titles of Related Interest

Dewar INDUSTRY VITALIZATION: Toward a National Industrial Policy
Hill/Utterback TECHNOLOGICAL INNOVATION FOR A DYNAMIC ECONOMY
Lundstedt/Colglazier MANAGING INNOVATION: The Social Dimensions of Creativity
Perlmutter/Sagafi-nejad INTERNATIONAL TECHNOLOGY TRANSFER
Sagafi-nejad/Moxon/Perlmutter CONTROLLING INTERNATIONAL TECHNOLOGY TRANSFER
Sagafi-nejad/Belfield TRANSNATIONAL CORPORATIONS, TECHNOLOGY TRANSFER AND DEVELOPMENT

Related Journals*

BULLETIN OF SCIENCE, TECHNOLOGY AND SOCIETY
COMPUTERS AND INDUSTRIAL ENGINEERING
COMPUTERS AND OPERATIONS RESEARCH
SOCIO-ECONOMIC PLANNING SCIENCES
TECHNOLOGY IN SOCIETY
WORK IN AMERICA INSTITUTE STUDIES IN PRODUCTIVITY

*Free specimen copies available upon request.

Understanding R&D Productivity

edited by
Herbert I. Fusfeld
Richard N. Langlois

The Technology Policy and Economic Growth Series,
Herbert I. Fusfeld and Richard R. Nelson, Editors

Published in cooperation with the Center for Science and Technology
Policy, Graduate School of Business Administration, New York University.

Pergamon Press
New York   Oxford   Toronto   Sydney   Paris   Frankfurt

197296

658.57
U 55

Pergamon Press Offices:

U.S.A.   Pergamon Press Inc., Maxwell House, Fairview Park,
                    Elmsford, New York 10523, U.S.A.

U.K.   Pergamon Press Ltd., Headington Hill Hall,
                    Oxford OX3 0BW, England

CANADA   Pergamon Press Canada Ltd., Suite 104, 150 Consumers Road,
                    Willowdale, Ontario M2J 1P9, Canada

AUSTRALIA   Pergamon Press (Aust.) Pty. Ltd., P.O. Box 544,
                    Potts Point, NSW 2011, Australia

FRANCE   Pergamon Press SARL, 24 rue des Ecoles,
                    75240 Paris, Cedex 05, France

FEDERAL REPUBLIC Pergamon Press GmbH, Hammerweg 6
OF GERMANY   6242 Kronberg/Taunus, Federal Republic of Germany

Copyright © 1982 Pergamon Press Inc.

Library of Congress Cataloging in Publication Data

Main entry under title:

Understanding R&D productivity

(Technology policy and economic growth series)
"Published in cooperation with the Center for
Science and Technology Policy, Graduate School of
Business and Administration, New York University."
Bibliography: p.
Includes index.
1. Research, Industrial. 2. Technological innova-
tions. 3. Industrial productivity. I. Fusfeld, Herbert I.
II. Langlois, Richard N. III. Title: R and D productivity.
IV. Series.
T175.U48   1982   658.57   82-12205
ISBN 0-08-028836-7

The editors gratefully acknowledge the support of the Alfred P. Sloan
Foundation, without which this book would not have been possible.

Printed in the United States of America

Contents

CHAPTER

Preface

The phrase "R&D productivity" embodies a large part of our conception of modern industry. "Productivity" - getting more output with less input - is the older notion, an icon of the industrial revolution that has inspired both the industrialist who sought it and the social critic who despised it. "R&D" - research and development - is of more recent import, capturing the modern association of science and technology with industry.

As one might expect from so heavily laden a phrase, our understanding of R&D productivity is a complex and incomplete one. More correctly, perhaps, we have many different conceptions of what R&D productivity means and many different formulas for its achievement; each of these visions adds an element to our overall understanding. There is no single unified theory of R&D productivity, no agreed-upon method of analyzing it, no unique approach to increasing it. But in the intelligent juxtaposition of diverse perspectives there can arise a coherent portrait of the state of our understanding of this important and far-reaching topic.

And therein lies the purpose of this volume: to present just such a set of perspectives, to assemble the views of some of the foremost students and practitioners of research and development.

Each of the chapters that follow was first presented at a seminar series organized by the Center for Science and Technology Policy at New York University during the spring semester of 1981. The participants include well-known academic and government scholars from several disciplines, along with top business executives responsible for the actual planning and conduct of industrial R&D.

Now, one can understand the topic "R&D productivity" in two ways: as concerned with the productivity of R&D itself -

as, for example, in an industrial laboratory - or as concerned with the import of R&D for overall industrial or economic productiveness. It was the first of these that we charged our speakers with exploring. But we knew from the start that the two sub-topics are ultimately inseparable; and you will see that our authors have ranged widely in both cases.

Here's a preview.

In the first chapter Herbert Fusfeld provides an introduction to the issues of R&D productivity. He suggests a way of viewing the problem and sets forth the questions that need to be answered.

The next chapters tackle the vexing problems of measurement. Charles Falk and Roberta Balstad Miller offer their thoughts on the conceptual and practical problems of data collection and interpretation.

Economics provides another view. Richard Nelson shows us how an economist - albeit a somewhat heterodox one - looks at R&D productivity and its relation to economic growth. And Richard Levin takes a close-up look at R&D productivity in the semiconductor industry, suggesting that, although a slackening in that industry's phenomenal rate of technical change is inevitable, the slowdown may not be as near as many people think.

Both William Abernathy and D. Bruce Merrifield examine the relationship of R&D productivity to corporate planning and management strategy. Abernathy elaborates on his controversial thesis that management style and outlook must bear much of the blame for a relative decline in the innovativeness of American industry. By contrast, Merrifield assigns inflation a greater role in the current problems of industry; but he echoes Abernathy's view that R&D and corporate planning should be more fully integrated, and he provides us with a positive vision of the future.

Another set of concerns take shape from the perspective of those concerned with the management of R&D laboratories. Lowell Steele takes us through the many considerations that enter into the evaluation of R&D projects in a commercial setting. And Arthur Anderson deals with the often-overlooked problem of improving an R&D system that is already functioning well.

In the penultimate chapter, Arthur Damask brings a physicist's ingenuity and thoroughness to the question of R&D productivity. The first half of his paper catalogues some of the empirical laws of productivity proposed through the centuries, while the second half presents a bold attempt to apply the mathematics of information theory to the problems of R&D management.

Finally, Alfred Nissan surveys all that came before, and concludes that the problems of R&D productivity discussed in these essays remain unsolved and manifestly complex. In a

brief afterword, Herbert Fusfeld offers a more upbeat coun-
terpoint to Nissan's conclusion, suggesting some reasonable
courses that might be pursued.

The editors would like to thank the authors of the chapters in this volume for taking the time from their busy sche-
dules to participate in the seminar series and to prepare their
remarks for publication. We would also like to thank Barbara
Muench for helping to organize the seminars, Shawn Roberts
for typing the manuscript in a truly professional manner, and
Carlos Santiago for rendering elegantly many of the diagrams.
The task of preparing the seminar materials for publication was
supported by a grant from Alfred P. Sloan Foundation - a
grant without which this volume would not have been possible
and for which we are extremely grateful.

1

Introduction: An Initial Approach to Understanding and Improving R&D Productivity

Herbert I. Fusfeld

PHILOSOPHICAL BASIS

I would like to introduce this subject on a personal note. During 25 years in industrial research, I have probably visited between 150 and 200 laboratories. After several hours at a location, following brief discussions with senior management and research staff, talking with more junior researchers about their programs, observing the nature of the research facilities and the level of activity, I would come away with a general impression as to whether that laboratory was a "productive" unit.

This was a highly subjective feeling since there were few, if any, quantitative data about performance. Nothing was measured or counted. On what basis could I arrive, rightly or wrongly, at a judgment about the "productivity" of the laboratory? There were obviously some clues in the statement of objectives, the sense of priorities, the sense of morale among those carrying out the research, the relationships within the laboratory and, in the case of industrial laboratories, between the laboratory and other parts of the corporation.

None of these is a direct measure of output. I probably assumed certain correlations, particularly for industrial research. First, good communication within the corporation plus a sense of priorities implies that technical progress in research would very likely be exploited by the corporation. Second, good morale within the laboratory implies a sense of security that normally relates to acceptance of the individuals, the laboratory, and their programs.

In short, I was not looking at the laboratory as an isolated unit, but as an integral part of a larger system. The

1

functioning of the laboratory can only be judged by the values and objectives of the system in which it exists and by which it is strongly conditioned. I believe this statement should hold equally for industry, government and the university. There are obviously arguments to be advanced about judging technical progress in an absolute sense. I believe this is a more sophisticated refinement of the general theme that research exists within a structure, although that structure can be private or public, corporate or academic.

Let me pursue this approach one further step. Anyone who has had the responsibility as director of a research laboratory is aware of the many management decisions involved. It is not simply a matter of hiring good researchers, however we judge that; arranging for good housekeeping; and watching for results. There are options as to organizational structure; allocation of resources by programs; allocation of resources among professionals, technicians, and equipment; decisions as to starting or stopping programs; and, particularly, forms of communication between the laboratory and the rest of the system. The point is that any research director believes that he can improve the effectiveness or "productivity" of the laboratory, and the preceding list of options shows some of the tools available to do so.

This brings us back to the problem of R&D productivity. When people believe that the performance of an organization or a system can be improved, one would expect that performance can be defined and hence measured. We are all aware that changes in structure, in priorities, and in resource allocation occur constantly in laboratories throughout government, industry and the university. Words such as improved "effectiveness" and "productivity" are invoked to support such changes. Yet definitions, consensus, and measurements are curiously missing.

Admittedly there is a value judgment, a subjective aspect, in results from research and development that seems to defy easy quantitative formulas for R&D productivity. So be it. The answers will not be easy and they may not be precisely quantitative in an arithmetical sense. Nevertheless, if we can sense that one laboratory is more "productive" than another, if we believe we can take actions to improve the "productivity" of a given laboratory, then we should be able to discuss, analyze and describe the basis for these judgments. Such descriptions should be a first step in identifying criteria for R&D productivity. This would permit evaluation, if not measurement. An understanding of these criteria might then suggest quantities that are measurable and relate to criteria that define R&D productivity.

The remainder of this chapter will suggest a conceptual approach that may provide a few initial steps to this difficult, critical, yet common obstacle to deriving optimum benefits from the truly massive dedication of resources in this country and internationally to science and technology.

STATEMENT OF THE PROBLEM

Considering the United States alone, about $69 billion will be spent on R&D activities in 1981, of which $34 billion will come from the private sector and almost all of the remainder from the federal government.* The ultimate output from this effort will appear to the world outside the R&D community in the form of new products, new processes, new services, and an increase in the reservoir of basic science and engineering. Can we increase the results flowing from this very considerable effort?   Can we obtain the same results with fewer dollars?

This broad spectrum of total national technical effort is simply too complex to evaluate as a single system, or to improve in a single approach.   The other extreme of considering a single laboratory unit, while it is a necessary first step, would not provide adequate insight about the relationships within the technical community.

I therefore propose to take as a first major objective consideration of the productivity of those R&D activities concerned with the civilian sector.   While in the United States this is primarily the $34 billion of industrial research, it is also intended to include those efforts within government and university laboratories whose results could normally be expected to benefit society through traditional economic mechanisms.

In the preceding section, I commented that we judge the work of a laboratory in terms of its role in a larger system. Hence, for our purposes, that larger system is the civilian sector.   The principal technical activities and responsibilities for the generation, conversion and integration of science and technology into our economic lives lies with the industrial research structure.   Keeping this in mind, the relevant activities of government and university that affect the civilian sector can be considered primarily in terms of their support for, and interaction with, industrial research.

What then will we be examining with this picture in mind? The line of reasoning I would suggest follows this pattern:

1. The overall objective is to derive the optimum benefits for the civilian sector from the ongoing investments in R&D.

---

*National Science Foundation, Science Indicators - 1980 (Washington, D.C., NSB-81-1).

2. The principal instrument for developing these benefits is the industrial research structure.
3. The system we will be examining can be considered in several broad functional categories of industrial research activity:

   a. Internal operations of industrial research organizations.
   b. Linkages between the industrial research structure and overall industry operations that determine the conversion and use of technology as products and services.
   c. Linkages between the industrial research structure and the external world of science and technology, consisting of university and government R&D activities as well as the additions to the technical reservoir coming from industrial advances throughout the world.

4. Special note should be taken of the processes by which government and university research activities intended for the civilian sector are initiated and linked to the system of economic use, since these can critically affect both the available technical reservoir and the stimulation of socially desired industrial activities.

If one were to describe this system with a diagram, it would not be a simple flow in a straight line from technical reservoir to industrial research to manufacture and use. My picture of the system we are considering is more like that of a large number of individual technical organizations floating in a sea of technology. This sea rests within an economic and social structure that determines the direction and magnitude of the technological flow, establishing constraints and pressures. There are infinite interactions and boundary conditions.

From this complex structure of our society, we can extract the activities most likely to generate and convert science and technology for the benefit of that society, and we can identify most of the critical factors that affect this process. Any system we define will be incomplete. Nevertheless, if we can understand and improve the system we define, we can expand it steadily to approach real-life conditions.

SUGGESTED CONCEPTS FOR CONSIDERATION

Since our emphasis is on the productivity of R&D intended for the civilian sector, a first approach to the necessary value judgments should be based upon the benefits perceived by the non-specialist in that sector. To be specific, we could focus on the judgments of the taxpayer, but that would imply a quantitative evaluation that is premature for this stage of study.

Suppose we could consider all relevant technical activities - industry, government and university - as being conducted within a "black box." How would the typical resident of the civilian sector view the "box?"

What goes into the "box" is relatively clear - money and people. But what comes out depends on what we are expecting, and the time scale can be critical. In simple terms, the civilian sector can observe, count, and partially evaluate new products, new processes and new services emerging from the "black box." The products and services are visible to the general public. Processes are less visible, since they form part of the corporate operations in manufacturing or services; but they are identifiable and can be evaluated in terms of lower costs, manufacturing productivity, and so on.

A fourth category of output is the increased reservoir of basic science and engineering. While this is not yet a tangible benefit for the civilian sector, it is a form of asset, a potential technical wealth, and must be included in order to achieve reasonable balance between inputs and outputs even in a descriptive sense. In this area, some kinds of judgments by a scientific peer group will clearly have to be developed and accepted by the nonspecialist.

Putting aside for the moment these additions to the technical reservoir, the general public sees products, processes, and services. It does not see as a current benefit such quantities as patents, articles, reference citations, and the like. These quantities remain in the black box. The possible use of such secondary or proxy quantities may provide clues to the health of our overall technical enterprise, but it requires specialists to interpret such secondary measures and to correlate them with the more tangible outputs.

As I have chosen to define the system, certain features stand out. For example, we can identify several areas for study which affect "productivity." A direct attempt to seek improvement might lead to definitions or evaluations of output from any consensus that emerges. The areas for consideration are:

1. Processes and criteria for selecting research programs. Technical results that do not reach society remain inside the black box. Industrial laboratories include economic disciplines to regulate the probable integration of R&D into business operations. Hence, the difficulties of choosing the "right" problems apply most heavily to government sponsored research and, less directly, to university research.

2. Transfer processes among technical sectors. Our concern is with ultimate benefits derived from the overall R&D system. The output of a single industrial laboratory can be based upon, and is usually influenced by, specific government and university research activities plus worldwide technical

advances from all sectors. The mechanisms for transfer via traditional professional activities, organized information systems, and specific cooperative arrangements are important to R&D productivity.

3. Effectiveness of individual laboratory R&D operations. There is constant pressure to allocate given resources for the optimum output. Since each laboratory has unique objectives and values, the most constructive general activity is to develop references for comparison and self-improvement. This calls for consensus as to important factors, and identification of differences between technical sectors and among separate industries.

I have suggested the "black box" concept of R&D as viewed by the average citizen in order to develop some sense of outputs. Many refinements will come to mind as we consider the details. There is the need to set up a separate evaluation for increases in our basic technical reservoir. There is the need to consider the economic impact of specific developments. There is increasing pressure to evaluate contributions to health, safety and the environment. There are real values in prestige that affect foreign policy, and thus our ultimate well-being.

The pragmatic concept of tangible output is then only a simplified first step. Still, it is understandable, and therefore can permit us to progress to more sophisticated levels.

APPROACHES TO THE PROBLEM

First understanding, then optimizing, a complex system calls for many contributions. A number of parallel approaches are clearly possible and desirable. It is only important that all approaches deal with the same system; therefore, I have repeated my own concepts in somewhat elementary detail.

Different approaches can be identified in terms of their content. Several examples to be considered are:

By Function

1. Direct Improvement. This has been discussed in the preceding section. Admittedly, there is a slightly illogical aspect to considering improvements in something not yet well-defined or measurable. But this is precisely what is done regularly in every research organization. Keeping in mind the broader objectives, an orderly analysis of such improvements may provide agreement on the nature of outputs and of value judgments. This is the focus for practitioners of research management.

2. <u>Economic Impacts</u>. Every new product, process, or service has an economic value, and we should eventually be in a position to define and estimate that value. It is different for the institution funding the R&D, for the user, and for society as a whole. This is the primary field of study for economic scholars like E. Mansfield, R.R. Nelson and others.

3. <u>Measurements</u>. Agreement on outputs is one of the ultimate results of a systematic approach to R&D productivity. Still, there is value in preparing a basis for discussion concerning (a) the significance of quantities that we do measure, and (b) the nature of quantities that can be measured. Several types of quantities that can be considered, to be discussed in more detail at the end of this section, include:

1. Identifiable outputs

2. Proxy or secondary indices

3. Characteristics of R&D operations

4. Technological progress functions.

Some relevant data are reported by the Commerce Department and the Science Resources Division of the National Science Foundation. The latter would be the more directly concerned with identified and measurable indices relating to this subject.

By Structure

1. <u>Industrial research within a single corporation</u>. The objectives, expectations and outputs within a given company should serve to provide qualitative definitions of productivity. History of change and efforts at improvement would strengthen definitions.

2. <u>Industrial research within a single industry</u>. Examining the origin and nature of technical change within a particular industry should broaden our view of both inputs and outputs. We would expect a perspective on R&D productivity for an industry to be different from that for a single company. This larger perspective could include such cooperative efforts as trade association research.

3. <u>External R&D related to a single industry</u>. Research within government and university laboratories that is intended to support a particular industrial area should be studied in conjunction with separate studies of that area. The evaluation of outputs would then combine both the technical progress of

the research organizations involved and the eventual integration of that progress within the industrial sector. The role and effectiveness of planning, of communication, and of transfer would all be factors in overall sector R&D productivity.

Throughout any of these approaches, there will be a sensitivity to quantities that are both measurable and meaningful. Therefore, I would like to comment a bit on the two categories referred to under "measurements" - namely, characteristics and technological progress functions.

By characteristics, I refer to quantities that tell us something about the scale and nature of a research organization. They are a form of input measurement, but tell us something about the procedures used in exploiting R&D. For example, the cost per professional person for operating a laboratory is an indicator of the mix of personnel and investment in capital facilities. The number alone is not significant, but differences within an industry and the trends over time can be. Similarly, the percentage of basic research as a function of laboratory size, the capital investment per research professional, and the ratio of engineers to scientists are all characteristics whose trends may offer possible clues to the sources of technical change and the probability of conversion to use. They are not outputs and they will not measure R&D productivity, but further studies of their importance may suggest directions for improvement.

Technological progress functions or performance functions may serve as indicators of advances in a particular industrial sector or technical field. Since such advances are the result of contributions from numerous sources (many contributions are not easily attributable) there may be no possible way to derive any estimate of R&D productivity from these quantities. Nevertheless, studies of possible correlations may be fruitful.

Such quantities can include, for example, a physical property such as the strength-to-weight ratio of alloy steels or the communication capacity per square millimeter of optical fiber, or they can refer to performance characteristics of a technological system such as the speed of aircraft, miles per gallon per 1,000 pounds of automobile, or bushels of wheat produced per acre. These quantities may have a relationship to the number of relevant articles published or the number of professional personnel employed in related fields. There has also been some correlation demonstrated between these technical characteristics and the relevant cumulative production (e.g., speed of aircraft related to total number of aircraft built). Technological progress functions of this sort are a form of output, despite the poorly defined inputs and the indefinite boundaries of the system. Nevertheless, these functions may provide new insights into the technical progress aspects of R&D productivity.

This chapter has attempted to discuss some facets of R&D productivity within the system of civilian-sector R&D. Following will be chapters presenting economic and social evaluations of R&D that raise some far more complex issues about what to evaluate as ultimate outputs. The significance and limitations of current measurements - and specifications for needed new measurements - will be reviewed. There will also be a general approach to the evaluation of industrial research. And the role of management and organizational structure will be discussed.

These chapters should provide some sense of where we stand in this field, what investigations and approaches appear most likely to yield further understanding, and what we might do to obtain measures of useful outputs. Finally, further investigations should suggest mechanisms for improving the overall R&D productivity of the system, or at least offer some consensus on how we can judge when the system has been improved.

The sum of these chapters is intended to provide a basis for the steady exploration of this critical field. It should affect directly the expenditures of very large sums of money and the efforts of much of the technical community. More important, the ultimate outputs of R&D impact directly upon our overall industrial productivity and quality of life. These are the underlying objectives of any improvement in the R&D system itself.

2

The Measurement of the Productivity of Science and Technology

Charles E. Falk

PERSPECTIVE

Science and technology have had an increasingly pervasive influence on almost every aspect of human affairs. Consequently, it is not too surprising that increasing resources have been devoted to the pursuit of science and technology, accompanied by a growing belief that science and technology are likely to have major beneficial effects on the society that develops them.

As both costs and expectations have escalated, more and more questions are being raised about the effectiveness of technical activities. Although not always put in these terms, the questions basically revolve around two related concepts – productivity and impact. Productivity refers to the effectiveness or efficiency of technical efforts and, following the economic concept of productivity, is usually measured in terms of outputs of scientific and technical activities in relation to the inputs that are provided. The impact issue does not deal so much with the efficiency of the technical processes, but involves the assessment of the effects, both beneficial and deleterious, of such activities.

Despite the relative ease of making subjective judgments on the nature and trends of science and technology productivity, objective assessments are usually preferable, and should be based as much as possible on quantitative information on inputs, outputs, and impacts. The measurement of these entities, their use and limitations, and the availability or absence of pertinent data are the focal topics of this paper.

"R&D and productivity" is the principal theme of these chapters. This chapter deals, however, with the somewhat broader concept of science and technology, since, certainly at

10

national and public levels, the issues mentioned above are most frequently raised with respect to these more comprehensive entities. Furthermore, the outputs of R&D are generally translated into impacts through other elements of the science and technology activity spectrum. This point can be demonstrated by the fact that, on a full time-equivalent basis, only about 25 percent of U.S. scientists and engineers are engaged in R&D activities.

Before discussing the specifics of quantitative information, it is important to consider statistical data in the proper perspective; without a clear understanding of their limitations, quantitative indicators can easily be misused. Thus, one should realize that such indicators are no panacea; for a variety of reasons, they will not by themselves solve all or even most decision-making problems. In the first place, the state of the art is still in its infancy, and many more years of conceptual development, research, and data-generation are required. Secondly, not all aspects of the science and technology system can be quantified at this time, or possibly ever. Examples are the quality of working scientists and engineers or the daringness and innovativeness of technical efforts. Thirdly, the system under examination is complex, since it is operating under the influence of many interactive forces. Often, adequate methodologies are not available to disentangle these causal features or to identify the effect of single factors. Quantification can also be limited by lack of data. There are various reasons for such deficiencies: the costliness of information collection; the reluctance of sources to provide data; the absence of time series which cannot be recreated.

Users of science and technology indicators should be aware of these types of limitations and should also realize that, as in any other activity, one type of tool is generally insufficient by itself for the resolution of a problem. Unawareness of such limitations will lead to overexpectations, frustrations, and disappointments. Quantitative measurements do represent a very useful tool for policy makers when such measurements are used within their limitations and in conjunction with other tools as well as with one exceedingly important ingredient - judgment.

Keeping these limitations and the role of quantitative indicators in mind, let us briefly examine input, output, and impact measures. Since a summary of available measurements would be much too time consuming, this review will concentrate on the gaps in the system. One should remember that a single statistic or even a single statistical time-series frequently is not an adequate indicator of the status of any significant element of the science and technology scene. Generally, a number of measures are required, including combinations of data and statistics. For example, data on patents are frequently used as a measure of technology output. Most would agree that the output to which patent data are fundamentally related is technical innovation. Yet there would also probably be agreement that patents measure only one phase of the innovation process, namely invention, and that many additional steps are required before invention can be converted to innovation. Thus, using patent data by itself does not provide us with a sufficiently good measure of innovative activity. Nevertheless, when used in conjunction with other types of information that illuminate other phases of the innovative process, patent data may lead to some general conclusions about the status of innovation.

INPUT MEASURES

While it is true that input measures are more numerous and more clearly defined than output or impact indicators, this should not be interpreted to mean that no problems or gaps exist on the input side. All too frequently, this group of indicators is considered adequate merely because rather broad and extensive data bases exist. Most of the available input measures deal with funding or the magnitude and characteristics of scientific and technical personnel. Even these sets of measures show significant gaps when evaluated, either in rather broad terms or from the point of view of specifics. Thus, funding information is limited to that involving research and development for which a rather comprehensive data base exists. Yet, R&D covers only one subset of scientific and technical activities. For those activities that lie beyond the R&D phase, such as production and dissemination, there are essentially no aggregate funding data. The same is true for what is frequently described as scientific and technological services, which encompass activities such as the generation, storage, and dissemination of scientific and technical information; routine measurements and observations; testing and standardization; routine analyses; etc. Thus, it is clear that by considering funding alone we are covering only one part of the system, a part that does not even represent the largest component.

In addition to these rather broad gaps, we also have some specific voids in our R&D funding data. For example, R&D support information is not quite complete because there are a few omissions, such as departmentally funded research carried out in academia and intramural research performed by state and local governments. Fortunately, estimates suggest that these omissions represent less than two percent of total U.S. R&D expenditures.

Disaggregated subelements of R&D funding data are also not always available. For example, while good data exist on the funding of academic R&D and basic research, it has not been possible up to now to obtain from universities information on their basic research expenditures in specific fields of science. Similarly, the National Science Foundation is just now attempting to obtain disaggregated industrial R&D funding data for such important crosscuts as: function, e.g., health, defense, transportation; R&D with long-term objectives versus R&D focusing on shorter-term goals; R&D directed toward the development of new products versus R&D directed toward the development of new processes. Furthermore, data on single companies are rather soft from a conceptual consistency point of view when they are obtained from Securities and Exchange Commission (form 10-K) filings; when these data are obtained in the NSF-Census surveys, they are confidential and cannot be made available. Much more quantitative input information is also required on the extent, magnitude, use and obsolescence of research equipment, considerations currently at the focus of a major national science policy issue.

For the other principal input-measure category, scientific and technical personnel, a much broader data base is in existence, at least in the United States. All scientists and engineers are covered by the information system, regardless of the nature of their work activity. Extensive information on numbers as well as on demographic, work, and professional characteristics is on hand.

Once again, some gaps exist. Except for industrial employment data, there is relatively little information on technicians, who represent an important input to technical programs. Furthermore, very little quantitative information is available on the quality of technical personnel or on its effectiveness in scientific and technological activities. Test scores, such as those resulting from the Graduate Record Examination or distributions by highest educational degree, are almost the only quantitative measures available. Yet these provide information only on the quality of students still in the educational pipeline or on new graduates. Yet quality, after several years of experience or measured in terms of effectiveness in real world situations, is probably an indicator for which there is a greater need. Clearly, for any complete assessment of productivity the quality of the inputs and outputs is just as important as their quantity. Quality considerations can be especially important in international comparisons of technical efforts when measured in terms of personnel. Thus, some countries have more scientists and engineers per 10,000 population than others, yet their technical efforts are not nearly as effective as those of countries with lower technical intensities because the quality of their scientists and engineers is lower.

There are other input aspects for which no quantitative data are available at all, even though these inputs play a very important role in determining the productivity and effectiveness of the system. Examples of such factors are the differ-

ential impact of the institutions in which science and technology are carried out, the environment in which science and
technology operate, and the extent to which these environments hinder or further technical efforts. Regulations,
controls, and working conditions all play an important role,
since they affect the morale of personnel and thus its efficiency.

OUTPUT MEASURES

The shortcomings of input measures appear relatively mild
when compared to the problems posed by the measurement of
outputs. Here coverage is much more sporadic.
    Two factors are principally responsible for the paucity of
output indicators. First, it is hard even to measure the quantity of outputs like new products and processes because of (a)
the difficulty in defining them and (b) the inability of institutions to keep track of such outputs. These obstacles are
compounded by qualitative considerations, since new products
and processes vary tremendously in social or economic value.
Furthermore, many process innovations are not radically new
but involve small incremental changes which frequently go
almost unnoticed. Similarly, many new products really involve
only minor changes in performance characteristics. A second
difficulty has been alluded to before, namely the fact that most
outputs are the product of several different types of activity,
and it is difficult to distinguish the role of science and technology. If innovations are defined as new products and processes that have been successfully introduced commercially,
their success depends not only upon science and technology
but also, for example, on marketing.
    Paradoxically, the output of one of the most subjectively
defined science and technology activities is one which up to
now has been most easily measured. I am referring to the
output of basic research. Since the primary objective of this
research is the development of new knowledge, and since the
type of knowledge involved is generally not subject to proprietary constraints, the announcement of such new knowledge is
an excellent output indicator measure. Thus, bibliometrics,
involving analyses of publication and citation counts, can provide a fairly good indication of both the quality and quantity
of basic research output. Furthermore, since publications and
citations can be counted relatively easily, a comprehensive
computerized data base has already been developed which has
been used extensively to measure basic research output.
Current bibliometric studies incorporate quite sophisticated
analyses to identify and overcome inherent methodological
difficulties.

When one moves to the more applied activities, one finds other useful output indicators such as the number and characteristics of patents and innovations. As mentioned previously, every one of these output measures is partial at best. Also, there are practically no data on the increasingly important phenomenon of technology transfer, whether measured in terms of human resources, mobility, capital investment, sales, or any other mechanism. As a matter of fact, there is still great confusion with respect to the definition of technology transfer, and too frequently attempts are made to measure this phenomenon through information transfer surrogates. But information transferred without the application of new knowledge does not constitute technology transfer.

Technical performance parameters constitute another set of output measures, which when viewed superficially seem to be related solely to technical activity. Examples of these are: the speed and capacity of transportation vehicles; the characteristics of materials; the speed and capacity of computers; the potency of pharmaceuticals; etc. This is an area which has just begun to be explored. Unfortunately, the more one examines the time patterns of these technical parameter changes, the more it becomes evident that nontechnical factors can again play a significant role. Thus, strategic economic and market factors can either accelerate or retard development or, at least, the introduction of new products with improved performance characteristics. Companies may hold back new developments if they endanger appropriate returns on previously developed products. Similarly, the degree of market saturation may prevent new product development or release. The technical capability for improved performance is a necessary but not a sufficient factor, and one has to be very careful in interpreting performance changes, since they may not properly reflect the current status of science and technology. Nevertheless, analysis of technical performance change shows a lot of promise and could provide one of the best measures of technical output.

As must be evident from this brief review, the classes of good output measures and the interpretation of specific output indicators are still quite limited. Furthermore, their relationship to the inputs that produce them is at best tenuous. There is, however, a tremendous demand for new and better output indicators, and any productive work in this area will continue to find a receptive clientele.

IMPACT MEASURES

Finally, let me turn to what are probably the most complex measures related to the output of science and technology

(S&T), namely those involving the impacts of the outputs. (These measures are frequently classified as output measures, even though they really do not fall conceptually into this category.)

The impacts of a specific technical output can be quite different in various environments, and are frequently affected by non-technical factors. Like many other measures of this type, S&T impact indicators are most effective when used in a comparative mode. Such comparison can involve changes over time, or differences between countries or institutions at a given time.

Some of the impact indicators are related more directly to science and technology than others. For example, science and technology can have a direct, significant impact on a nation's trade and competitiveness in the international marketplace. Thus, the balance of trade in high technology products is frequently used as a science and technology impact measure, as is the balance of technological payments due to royalties and license fees. Other impact measures are related more indirectly to science and technology. One of these is productivity itself. Studies have shown again and again that science and technology play important roles in productivity growth. These same studies also reveal, however, that many other factors are significant in determining productivity levels.

There are numerous categories of social indicators that are partial science and technology impact measures. Examples include indicators of health, housing, and other measures of the standard of living. While it is sometimes relatively easy to develop such quantitative social indicators, it is generally quite difficult to interpret what the data show or measure with respect to the impact of science and technology. Better health, for example, can be due to sociological as well as technological factors.

SUMMARY

Obviously, it has only been possible in this chapter to skim through the nature and problems of measures related to the productivity and impact of science and technology. In summary, input data are currently in best shape, while output and impact measures are getting increasing conceptual attention and are in greatest demand. Since science and technology policy is diffused through every element of our society, questions about S&T effectiveness occur at almost every organizational level, ranging from individual research laboratories, companies, and academic institutions to such broader entities as localities, states, and nations. If this pervasiveness is coupled with the increased limitation of resources, it is not surprising that there is a large and growing interest in the development and production of quantitative measures that can aid in the assessment of science and technology productivity and impact, and thus in the allocation of available resources. Consequently, the field of science and technology indicators is not just intellectually challenging, it also fulfills a major need of the policy-formulation process.

3
Measurement Issues in R&D Productivity
Roberta Balstad Miller

In recent years there has been a growing interest in R&D productivity, stimulated both by concern over declines in the rate of industrial productivity and by conditions specific to R&D. The argument has been made that national productivity is, in fact, heavily dependent upon R&D productivity. R&D, according to this obviously simplified model, filters down from the basic research laboratory to the workplace, where technological innovations derived from basic scientific research are translated into increases in industrial productivity. The tie between technological innovation and productivity has been so widely accepted that productivity growth rates have been used as indicators of technological innovation.(1)

The validity of this model is questionable. As Nathan Rosenberg has pointed out, the United States sustained higher rates of productivity increase with lower levels of R&D expenditure prior to 1960 than it did after 1970. Moreover, the direction of influence is not fixed. Technological innovation frequently "filters up" to basic scientific research, as when improvements in instrumentation foster advances in basic research or when an industrial research laboratory, put in place for the "D" of R&D, begins to stimulate basic research as well.(2)

In addition, there are many non-technological influences on industrial productivity that are ignored in the model. These include, but are certainly not limited to, conditions of work, attitudes and skills of workers, the organization of the workplace, and the quality of the end product. The values and institutions of the society and the structure of the economy also strongly influence productivity. In short, national productivity is not merely a derivative of investments in R&D in the physical sciences and engineering. Moreover, if the Japanese experience can be a guide, increased R&D in the social and behavioral sciences would have a far more immediate effect on U.S. industrial productivity than R&D in the so-called hard sciences.(3)

Arguments linking R&D expenditures and industrial productivity are nonetheless important for two reasons. First, the study of industrial productivity suggests models for the development of indicators of productivity in science and technology. Second, a belief in the tie between the two influences the level and the distribution of research funds in the United States. One consequence of this belief has been the growing interest among policy makers in indicators of productivity in R&D.

There are other reasons as well for this interest. Demands for accountability in all areas of public expenditure have had an effect on appropriations for R&D. The post-Sputnik honeymoon of the American public with science and technology is clearly over, and scientists are increasingly asked to defend R&D expenditures against other public uses of funds.

Another explanation, represented by the recent publication of Scientific Productivity: The Effectiveness of Research Groups in Six Countries (edited by Frank M. Andrews and published by Cambridge University Press and UNESCO, 1979), is that the impulse to seek indicators of productivity is impelled less by the imperatives of accountability to funders than by a desire on the part of researchers to stretch scarce resources for R&D and to improve performance and efficiency in scientific research. In the private sector, research funds must encompass defensive as well as innovative research and may be increasingly used in the near future for productivity research, in addition to the more traditional R&D. The development of indicators of scientific productivity promises to clarify the definition and discussion of productivity in R&D, if not to resolve the underlying political and distributional problems.

In this chapter, I will look at the technical concept of productivity, examine what we know about productivity in R&D from available indicators, and then discuss conceptual and measurement problems in developing better indicators. I will argue that we cannot measure productivity in R&D in an absolute sense, but that there are still many benefits in attempting to do so; that we must not be content with current indicators of productivity, regardless of how good they are; and that we must both refine the input/output model for R&D productivity and move beyond it to develop models of productivity based on different values.

TECHNICAL PRODUCTIVITY

Industrial productivity, the indicator most frequently used when speaking of productivity, is generally calculated as output per hour of work performed. Technically, productivity is the ratio of measured outputs to measured inputs per unit of time. Interpreted broadly, productivity ratios incorporate all outputs, and both human and non-human inputs. In practice, input and output data are often difficult to obtain, and productivity ratios are constructed with the closest available approximations to total input and output.(4)

Both total aggregate productivity and productivity for various sectors of the economy can be calculated. These divisions can also be used in thinking about productivity in R&D, where total productivity could refer to R&D in the science and technology enterprises as a whole, and sector productivity refer to such areas of R&D as industrial, government, or university R&D; to fields in science and technology; or to research units, such as laboratories.(5)

DETERMINING OUTPUT

Measuring productivity in R&D is, at bottom, a problem in devising output indicators. We have input indicators in abundance - investments in R&D, investments in scientific and technological training, and employment of scientists and engineers, to name but a few. Output indicators are less fully developed. The U.S. Science Indicators reports rely principally upon patents and analyses of scientific and technical literature for some sense of the output of scientific and technological research. At the same time, the authors wisely caution the reader: "It is impossible to quantify precisely the results of research or determine the incremental advancement of knowledge provided by an increase in R&D funding."(6)

These indicators give us useful information on some of the outputs or products of science and technology over time. For example, publication of articles by U.S. scientists as a proportion of all articles published in 2,100 highly cited journals remained relatively constant from 1973 to 1977 (table 3.1). When disaggregated by field, however, these data show slight declines in the U.S. share of publications in most fields, with the exception of clinical medicine and biomedicine, and a larger decline in the proportion of articles in mathematics and biology. Because of the sizeable number of articles published in clinical medicine and biomedicine, the total U.S. proportion of articles remains relatively constant, and the decline in seven out of the nine fields is disguised in the aggregate figures.(7)

Table 3.1.   U.S. Proportion of the World's Articles:
1973-1977

Field	Percent		
	1973	1975	1977
All fields	39	38	38
Clinical medicine	43	43	43
Biomedicine	39	39	39
Biology	46	45	42
Chemistry	23	22	22
Physics	33	32	30
Earth and space sciences	47	44	45
Engineering and technology	42	41	40
Psychology	76	75	74
Mathematics	48	44	41

Source: National Science Foundation.   Science Indicators 1978.
(Washington, D.C.: Government Printing Office.)

Patent data, more an indicator of inventiveness than of the output of R&D, show declines in the number of patents granted to U.S. inventors and increases in U.S. patents granted to applicants from other nations.   Robert Evenson has calculated the ratio of U.S. patents to full-time scientists and engineers in the United States and to expenditures on R&D (table 3.2).   In both cases, the ratio declined from 1965 to 1977, suggesting a decline in the productiveness of U.S. science.   By separating industrial R&D from government R&D, he locates the source of the decline more precisely in industry. The industrial sector has higher ratios than the government. That is, for a given investment in R&D or scientific and engineering manpower, industry is more likely to apply for a patent than the government and, hence, is more "productive"

Table 3.2.   Output in Patents.

Patents Per Full Time Scientist and Engineer

	1965	1977
All Sectors	.102	.073
Industry	.103	.076
Government	.025	.023

Patents Per Million Dollars R&D (1972 Dollars)

	1965	1977
All Sectors	1.86	1.43
Industry	1.87	1.47
Government	.37	.35

Source: National Science Foundation. Science Indicators
          1978.   (Washington,   D.C.:   Government   Printing
          Office.)

in terms of patenting. Because these ratios are dropping
considerably faster for industry than for government research,
however, the difference between industry and government
ratios has declined over time.(8)
    Although these indicators can tell us about some of the
recent changes in the output of U.S. science and technology,
they are inadequate if they are the sole basis for indicators of
productivity. Productivity calculations should encompass a full
range of outputs. Confining measured output to publications
and patents ignores too many other significant outputs of R&D,
and as a consequence underrepresents total output and de-
presses the productivity ratio. Not only does this under-
estimate the actual productivity of scientific and technological
research, it also obscures changes in the efficiency and productiveness of R&D over time.
    A measure of R&D efficiency, one aspect of productivity,
has been suggested by Herbert I. Fusfeld as a supplement to
measures of output. Because expenditures for R&D are used
to support professionals, technicians, support staff, and

equipment, a comparison of the efficiency of R&D investment in government and industry can be obtained by looking at the cost per professional employee in each sector. These indicators can also be compared across time.(9)

A COMMON METRIC

Equally as important as the paucity of output indicators in hindering the construction of input-output productivity ratios for R&D is the absence of a common metric for the various inputs and outputs of science. For example, most indicators of scientific input are in reality measures of investment in R&D. Many of these can be expressed in economic terms - such as dollars spent on R&D or in support of scientific and engineering personnel, facilities, and instrumentation. Important long term inputs not readily expressed in dollar values include the training of new generations of scientists and engineers, the quality of that training and of ongoing research, and the satisfaction, energy, diligence, and creativity of those doing the research.

Output indicators are even more diverse and difficult to quantify or assign an economic value. As Stanley Engerman notes, it is conceivable in theory to apply hypothetical pricing schemes to the outputs of all scientific and technological R&D and thus reduce difficulties in aggregating such different kinds of output. Yet the more basic the research, the more difficult it has been to capture its benefits, particularly for a limited time period. In the face of this, molding the evaluation of basic research to fit an alien economic metric is both inaccurate and misleading.(10)

The same problem holds for measuring the impact of R&D on the economy and the society. Some estimates can be made of the social return to investment in R&D or to the economic effect of improvements in mortality and morbidity, manufacturing performance, and standard of living which result from technological advance. However, R&D-induced changes in individual behavior, working conditions, health, and life styles are not nearly so amenable to numerical summary and aggregation, much less to economic valuation.

Yet despite clear limitations in our ability to reduce all indicators to a common metric for use in the calculation of scientific and technological productivity, there are still benefits to be gained from thinking about the subject as if it were possible. These benefits do not necessarily include the calculation of productivity ratios for R&D according to the traditional economic formulas. Rather, discussion of conceptual and measurement issues in determining the productivity of R&D forces us to clarify our thinking about what it is that science and technology produce and how we might measure it. This, in turn, improves our ability to make cross-national and over-time comparisons of the relationships between scientific and technological productiveness and investments in R&D, in research personnel, and in the structure and organization of research.

There is another important reason for scientists and policy-makers to discuss this subject. One impetus for the current interest in the productivity of R&D is the growing scarcity of resources for research. Under these conditions, investments in R&D will increasingly be balanced against other types of investments, and arguments in support of R&D will be most successful if they show substantial public or private benefit from the R&D and productive and efficient use of each R&D dollar. Because of these pressures, productivity in R&D may well become a significant political issue. At that time, rather than having measures of productivity imposed from outside the scientific community, such measures should if at all possible be developed by scientists who are themselves close to the R&D process.

The problem of devising a metric for output indicators is but one of a number of conceptual and measurement problems in developing indicators of productivity in R&D. These include, at a minimum: (1) the absence of measures of the broad range of outputs of the R&D process; (2) our lack of understanding of the process by which inputs are transformed into outputs and of differences in that process within and across fields; (3) our lack of an analytically derived basis for determining intervals of observation in both input and output measures; and (4) our inability to account for the many elusive and difficult to quantify inputs to scientific productiveness and efficiency. These problems are closely related to each other. I shall discuss each of them in turn.

OUTPUT INDICATORS

The inadequacy of current indicators has already been raised. Yet if discussions of productivity in scientific and technological research and development are to consider a broader spectrum of outputs of that process, we need to identify the areas where output measures are needed. A basic taxonomy should, at the least, encompass outputs in the following areas:

1. basic scientific research;

2. technology and innovation;

3. research applied to product and process improvement;

4. social impacts (the economic, social, and individual effects
    of R&D).

A second, and more difficult, task is to develop indicators in each of these categories. In the first category, for
example, publications and patents citations can both be used to
give some indication of the output of scientific research. Both
are palpable, visible products of research. But the most
important product of scientific research, new knowledge, is
neither palpable nor visible. Indicators of influential scientific
advance and of the major economic, structural, and intellectual
forces that affect scientific research have been termed "qualitative indicators" by Gerald Holton, who argues that measures
of the quality of scientific research and the nonmonetary influences on the course of R&D are as important in evaluating the
output of science and technology as the more easily calculated
quantitative indicators.(11)
The fourth category of outputs, indicators of the influence of R&D on the society, have been perennially difficult to
develop. In the 1960s, NASA funded a study of the effects of
the space program on American society. Raymond Bauer and
his colleagues in the study concluded that these effects could
not be determined without better measures of change in the
society. They coined a name for the measures needed: social
indicators. Since then the field of social indicators has advanced considerably, but the problems that led to the call for
indicators are still with us. Measuring the social impacts of
R&D is complicated by the broad array of short- and long-term
influences of science and technology on individuals, institutions, and structures in the society as well as the direct and
indirect influence of scientific research on such factors as the
quality of life.(12)

PRODUCTIVITY AND THE R&D PROCESS

The second problem in measuring productivity is related to the
first. As Engerman points out, most analyses of productivity
using R&D expenditures as an input variable assume that inputs are invariant in their relationship to such outputs as
scientific advance or economic growth. This assumption is
usually coupled with the further assumption that the internal
structure of the R&D process is also invariant with respect to
the definition of productiveness.(13)
It would be more realistic to assume that inputs are converted into outputs at rates and by processes that differ from
field to field and, within fields, from discipline to discipline.
"Production" depends not only on the input resources, but
also on the efficiency and creativity with which they are used,

and the structure of scientific and technological problems in the field. Not only is the per-dollar payoff for R&D investment different in each field, but the processes by which R&D leads to desirable outcomes is highly variable and frequently unknown. Indeed, the very definition of what are inputs and outputs is dependent upon the definition of the research and the form of the desired outcome. For example, it is commonly supposed that research in basic science yields findings that are applicable to research in technology. The "development" of the findings of basic research, in turn, stimulates innovations in industry and growth in the economy. Yet it is possible for parts of the process to be reversed, as in the case of the early influence of mining and dyeing on metallurgy and chemistry, where the outputs of technology became inputs to science.

Discussions of the measurement of productivity must begin by recognizing that we know little about the process by which inputs are transformed into outputs and that productivity is dependent both upon definitions of significance which vary by field of research and upon the social and scientific utility of the outcomes of the research. In short, productivity in R&D is both a variable and a relative concept.

INTERVALS OF OBSERVATION

Most existing input indicators are made available on an annual basis - examples are resources for R&D, Ph.Ds granted in various fields of science, or scientists and engineers employed within and across sectors of the R&D enterprise. This is not surprising given that most of the data are obtained from institutions that calculate such figures annually for their own purposes. Moreover, for comparisons of data over time, an important factor in the study of indicators, the calendar year is a convenient and nearly universally recognized interval of comparison.

This complicates the development of indicators of productivity because output indicators (the other part of the input/output productivity equation) do not fit easily into the calendar-year framework. The problem is not that the data, if available, cannot be obtained annually. It is, rather, that annual changes in scientific and technological outputs are not directly related to annual changes in inputs. For example, the annual allocation of resources and personnel to R&D certainly affects the research enterprise. Yet, although changes in these inputs can modify and even halt research, the measurable annual resource and personnel inputs are only part of what is needed for productive research in science. Productive research requires more than simply placing a scientist in a laboratory.

As a result of internal institutional imperatives and, at time, inertia, the results of research do not fall out nicely in annual increments. Nor do they necessarily appear within any single larger or smaller time unit. The critical factor in productive R&D activities may, in fact, be related to institutional stability and be cumulative only after several years of inputs. This variable time lag between investment and production (partial input and output) in R&D becomes increasingly variable as we look beyond particular fields or research units to the national scientific system.

Despite these problems, the calculation of indicators of productivity requires some comparison of inputs to outputs. Given both the form of the available input data and past practice in reporting it in annual increments, such calculations are likely to be made on an annual basis. It should be understood, however, that the comparison of annual increments (or decrements) in input to annual increments (or decrements) in output is an imperfect indicator because the output in the equation is not directly related to the input. If indicators of scientific production and efficiency can be devised without directly relating outputs to inputs, the annual interval of the data might still pose a measurement problem, but not the analytical problem raised here.

PROBLEMS IN MEASURING INPUTS

Thus far, our discussions have focused on measures of output for R&D; but there are important problems to be resolved in the measurement of input as well before we can develop indicators of productivity in R&D.

Because of the continuing need to secure physical and economic resources for the conduct of R&D, discussions on productivity tend to center around those inputs to the research process. However, the recent study by Andrews and his colleagues found little relationship between indicators of funding and other material inputs to R&D, and the effectiveness of research units in six countries. More important to productiveness and efficiency were certain sociological, psychological, and organizational characteristics of the research unit. For example, the ability and personality of the director of the unit and the satisfaction of the researchers with their colleagues was central to productive research units.(14)

Unlike indicators of funding and employment, indicators of these subjective and often elusive qualities are not immediately available. Social scientists have developed means to measure some of the social and structural inputs, but obtaining indicators at the level of the research unit for every unit in the country would be prohibitively expensive. Obtaining indicators of social and structural factors through sampling from the total population of research units would perhaps be easier for a national research system, although it would be nonetheless expensive.

In technology, too, there are inputs which are difficult to quantify. These include, as Engerman terms it, "learning-by-doing" in the production process and "learning-by-using" in the development of new product capabilities. In addition to creating measurement problems, these inputs to technological R&D complicate the analysis of productivity still further because they first appear after the R&D process is well under-way, rather than at the beginning.(15)

NEXT STEPS

It is not wise to push this discussion of measurement problems to a set of firm recommendations on what indicators should be used to measure R&D productivity. The subject is, at present, too underdeveloped to close any avenue of approach by prematurely rejecting or institutionalizing particular measures of productivity. It is possible, however, to suggest promising directions for further discussion and research and issue a caveat or two to pioneer researchers in the field.

First, there is a need for improved and more inclusive measurement of both inputs and outputs of the research process. This is as much a research problem as a measurement problem. The full range of influences on R&D need first to be identified and then to be measured. Similarly, the outputs of the process - from new knowledge to changes in the living conditions of ordinary citizens - need to be defined. Because the search for a single metric is likely to be unproductive, measures of output should be developed in a variety of metrics. Analyzed separately and compared over time, these several indicators series can tell us more about productivity than we currently know or can learn from a single productivity indicator.

Second, we need continuing inquiry into measurement and conceptual problems in productivity indicators. It is not enough to develop a set of generally accepted indicators of productivity. Because of the epistemological problems discussed here and changes in what we expect from R&D, there will always be a need to improve or update our measures. If we do not do so, we run the risk of institutionalizing imperfect indicators of productivity and, in time, confusing the indicators themselves with productivity. Identifying R&D productivity with what we can measure may show that we have high (or low) productivity on paper, but it will not necessarily tell us much about the productiveness of R&D in a dynamic environment.

The problem is analogous to the measurement problem in determining economic productivity. Serious questions have been raised about whether the United States is experiencing a real decline in productivity, or whether our current indicators simply fail to capture productivity increases in the service sector. There is a danger that indicators of R&D productivity, if institutionalized, could similarly confine our concept of what constitutes productive R&D. For example, new products could be valued in indicator construction at the expense of improved production processes or techniques, or new knowledge at the expense of creative syntheses of what is already known. To guard against this, there should be a continuing focus on measurement and, since R&D takes place in a changing context over time, we should look to new indicators which reflect changing R&D needs to add to the arsenal of indicators we already have.

Third, the most effective use of indicators of R&D productivity is in a comparative framework. Our measures, imperfect as they are, will acquire meaning and significance when used to compare research systems over time and in different countries. As the National Academy of Science's Panel to Review Productivity Statistics observed in its report. "Productivity measures exist largely to be compared - we are interested almost exclusively in productivity differences or productivity changes." It is in this respect, finally, that the measurement of productivity in R&D perhaps most resembles the measurement of economic productivity.(16)

The current and growing interest in productivity in R&D and elsewhere should not lead us to equate productiveness and efficiency with value. Productivity is but one value; others are: the creation of new knowledge; the diffusion of beneficial technologies; and improvement of living conditions. Because the latter three will not always be accomplished productively and efficiently, the use of indicators of productivity in science and technology must be tempered by a recognition that the evaluation of science should not be based on a single type of indicator, such as productivity, but should be based on the needs and values of society itself.

NOTES

1. See John W. Kendrick, Understanding Productivity: An Introduction to the Dynamics of Productivity Change, Policy Studies in Employment and Welfare, No. 31 (Baltimore, 1977) and "Productivity Trends and Prospects," U.S. Economic Growth From 1976 to 1986: Prospects, Problems, and Patterns, Vol. 1, prepared for the Joint Economic Committee, U.S. Con-

gress (Washington, 1976); Mary Ellen Mogee, Technology and Trade: Some Indicators of the State of U.S. Industrial Innovation, prepared for the Subcommittee on Trade of the Committee on Ways and Means, U.S. House of Representatives (Washington, 1980); Science Indicators 1978 (Washington, 1979).

2. Nathan Rosenberg, "An Examination of International Technology Flows in Science Indicators 1978," unpublished paper, p. 3; Herbert I. Fusfeld, "Research Support - From Right to Left," Physics Today, November 1974, p. 104.

3. Kendrick, Understanding Productivity, p. 9; Robert E. Cole, "The Human Element in Economic Performance: The Role of the Social Sciences," Seminar on Research, Productivity and the National Economy, Committee on Science and Technology, U.S. House of Representatives, June 18, 1980 (Washington, 1980), pp. 47-53; Luther J. Carter, "Industrial Productivity and the 'Soft Sciences,'" Science 209:476-477.

4. Kendrick, Understanding Productivity, pp. 12-27; National Research Council, Panel to Review Productivity Statistics, Measurement and Interpretation of Productivity (Washington, 1979), pp. 19-49.

5. There is, in addition, a considerable literature on the productivity of individual scientists. See, for example, J. Scott Long, "Productivity and Academic Position in the Scientific Career," American Sociologial Review 43:889-908.

6. Science Indicators 1978, p. 14.

7. Science Indicators 1978, pp. 15-16, 150-151.

8. Robert Evenson, "Technology Indicators: Comments on SI 78," unpublished paper presented at the Review Symposium on Science Indicators 1978 sponsored by the Social Science Research Council's Subcommittee on Science Indicators, May 16, 1980.

9. Herbert I. Fusfeld, "Overview of U.S. Research and Development," in W.N. Smith and C.F. Larson, editors, Innovation and U.S. Research (Washington, 1980), pp. 3-19.

10. Stanley L. Engerman, "Measuring Science and Technology: Some Economic Questions," unpublished paper presented at the Social Science Research Council's Review Symposium on Science Indicators 1978, May 16, 1980.

11. Gerald Holton, "Can Science Be Measured?" in Yehunda Elkana, et al., editors, Toward a Metric of Science: The Advent of Science Indicators (New York, 1978), pp. 39-68. Essays in this book were first presented at a review symposium on Science Indicators 1972, jointly sponsored by the Social Science Research Council and the Center for Advanced Study in the Behavioral Sciences.

12. See Raymond A. Bauer, editor, Social Indicators (Cambridge, 1966); Edwin Mansfield, "R and D's Effects on Economic Performance," Seminar on Research, Productivity and the National Economy, pp. 12-16; and Harriet Zuckerman and Roberta Balstad Miller, "Indicators of Science: Notes and Queries," in Science Indicators: Implications for Research and Policy, Zuckerman and Miller, editors (Amsterdam, 1980), pp. 347-353. The papers presented in this volume, a special issue of Scientometrics, were first presented at the Social Science Research Council's Review Symposium on Science Indicators 1976.

13. Engerman, "Measuring Science and Technology."

14. Frank M. Andrews, editor, Scientific Productivity: The Effectiveness of Research in Six Countries (Cambridge and Paris, 1979).

15. Engerman, "Measuring Science and Technology."

16. National Research Council, Measurement and Interpretation of Productivity, p. 22.

4

R&D Productivity at the Economy-Wide Level

Richard R. Nelson

Herbert Fusfeld's chapter considered the meaning and deter-
minants of R&D productivity, primarily at the level of the
laboratory or firm. My chapter is directed toward considerations relevant to thinking about R&D productivity at the level
of the society or the economy. But before getting on with
that discussion, I, like Fusfeld, would like to call attention to
different connotations that might be carried by the term "research productivity." One connotation of "productive" is
"efficient," in the sense of well-organized, tidy, tightly
controlled, optimized. For reasons I will make clear, I do not
think this is a useful way of thinking about productivity of
R&D. Other connotations that I think more fruitful are "responsive" and "creative." By responsive I mean sensitive to
demands and needs, and appreciative of what kinds of breakthroughs and advances will have value. By creative I mean
ingenious and sophisticated in assessing alternative ways to
solve problems and achieve objectives.

Much of the literature on R&D project and program management is consonant with the latter point of view. It is
sensitivity to where the pay-offs are high and creativity in
thinking through approaches and in actually doing the R&D
work - not tidy administration or the sorts of decision procedures that would make an accountant happy - that receive the
emphasis in this literature.

R&D is inherently an untidy business; and effective R&D
management is in large part a matter of recognizing this and
making appropriate allowances. These considerations ought to
carry over when we think about R&D productivity at the eco-
nomy-wide level or about the institutions and policies that
"manage" our national R&D effort. It would be pernicious folly
to try to establish a national R&D plan and an administrative
structure to try to see that it gets carried out. Even the

Russians know this, although from time to time their top administrators forget about it. What one wants is an R&D system that is pluralistic, with diverse and independent decision centers, spurred and guided by incentives to do R&D that has social pay-off, in a creative and energetic manner. Our decentralized, competitive, market- and profit-oriented industrial R&D sector avoids many of these vices and has many of these virtues.

It should be recognized that our business R&D system is surely not tidy or efficient in any standard meaning of that term. It wastes R&D resources on projects of very little or perhaps even negative social value, and is neglectful of many areas of R&D that would have significant social payoffs. The key to the incentive system is appropriability, assured through nontrivial lead time or patent protection, or both. Even where markets for goods and services do accurately reflect social benefits and cost, the appropriability requirement and rivalry among firms distorts R&D incentives. When a rival can quickly or cheaply follow an innovator, there is not much profit in being an innovator, and not much less in not being one. On the other hand, if one firm comes up with a significantly new product or process, its competitors may be spurred to R&D efforts to essentially duplicate, or invent around, the innovator's proprietary technology - efforts that surely involve at least some element of social waste. Appropriability problems aside, markets for goods and services surely do not adequately reflect social benefits and costs in all dimensions. For many years, environmental degradation did not appear in the profit and cost accounting influencing private R&D decision making. Over the last decade or two, we have developed an elaborate regulatory structure aimed at influencing R&D decision making so that environmental costs are heeded. Virtually nobody would argue, however, that the system that has evolved for protecting environmental values is neat, efficient, or even very sensible.

Our system of corporate R&D surely is messy and inefficient, in the everyday sense of that term. Were God in charge here, she surely would not organize R&D that way. But humans are not gods. The system we have avoids certain follies, and has considerable virtues. Indeed, it may be difficult for anybody who is not God to improve upon it significantly. Effective thinking about R&D productivity requires appreciation of the weaknesses as well as the strengths of the existing system. It sure ain't perfect. But policy aimed to make it more tidy is unlikely to improve its performance.

Effective thinking also requires recognition that the current national system of R&D is a very mixed one. It includes much more than business firms making their own R&D decisions on the basis of their own profit calculations. It also includes governmental and nonprofit institutions that fund R&D and some that do R&D. There are even still some private freelance inventors around, at least in certain fields. As a first cut, one can think in terms of the following broad division of labor. Where the markets for a good or service are private and business firms have the capability and incentive to do R&D, applied R&D is largely left to the private sector. For basic scientific research and similar activities, where proprietary rights are difficult, or undesirable, to establish, universities are the primary locus of work and, since World War II, governmental funds provide the bulk of support. For goods and services that are largely public, or for which there is a strong public interest, governmental R&D funds also may be provided. The locus of the work may be business firms, government agencies, or universities.

But while the above roughly characterizes the prevailing division of labor, there are many exceptions. In particular, it is important to recognize significant differences across industries and technologies. These differences are striking enough that it may not make any sense to think of a national R&D system. Rather, the appropriate conceptual unit for analysis might better be the sector or the industry. Both the nature of the R&D and the institutional funding structure for R&D differ significantly between agriculture and aviation, between pharmaceuticals and civil aircraft, between education and semiconductors. I shall come back to some of these differences.

Herbert Fusfeld discussed several different ways to try to measure R&D productivity. I would like here to describe the approach many economists have taken to that problem. That method involves tracing growth of productivity (output per worker) in the economy as a whole, and in different industries over time, and trying to attribute a certain fraction of that to research and development spending. An important difficulty with that method is that, when the nature of final products changes significantly over time, it is not easy to devise an output measure that adequately recognizes changes in product characteristics. The trick is somehow to account for a significantly improved product as "more" product, so that, when the improvement is introduced, output per man goes up just as it would in the case of a simple efficiency-increasing innovation. The fact is that our output series in many cases do not adequately account for the appearance of new or better products. This is not to say that quality improvements never are adequately accounted, or that economists doing these studies are unaware of the problem. It is that the trick is very difficult to pull off.

What do the data show? At the macroeconomic level, they show that, since the 1920s at least, growth of output per worker in the United States has proceeded much faster than simple augmentation of capital equipment per worker, or of other changes that one could imagine as proceeding without R&D, would explain. The lion's share of the measured productivity growth we have experienced must be attributable to something like technological advance, and therefore to R&D and other expenditures behind those advances. If we could better account the worth of radically new products, measured technological advance surely would be even greater.

At the industry or sectoral level, the most striking phenomenon is the very great disparity across sectors in their rates of measured productivity growth and technological change. Sectors like civil aircraft production, semiconductors, and pharmaceuticals have experienced extraordinarily rapid rates of productivity growth and measured technological advance: Sectors like furniture production, residential construction, and education have experienced very low rates of productivity growth and measured technological advance. It is an interesting fact that the sectors experiencing rapid productivity growth have almost invariably been ones in which either firms in the industry, or the input and capital goods supplying firms, do a significant amount of research and development.

There have been a number of studies which have tried to assess the "productivity" of R&D in terms of the ratio of the enhanced market value flowing from R&D successes to R&D expenditures incurred - in effect, a benefit/cost analysis (in one form) or a rate of return calculation. With few exceptions, these studies have rested on some extremely troublesome assumptions. It is not clear, therefore, how seriously their conclusions ought to be taken. However, it should be noted that virtually all of these studies have shown R&D to be extraordinarily productive in the sense of very high benefit/cost ratios or rates of return.

To my mind, however, what is most striking about these kinds of studies is, as I suggested above, the enormous differences among economic sectors in rates of technical change experienced. Put another way, R&D has been dramatically productive in enhancing our ability to meet certain wants, but not others.

I wish to conclude on the following theme. This is a nation that makes much of its private, profit and market R&D system. In thinking about R&D productivity, however, perhaps we ought to recognize better than we have that in many of the economic sectors where we have experienced the most dramatic technological advances, government R&D support has played an extremely important role. Agriculture is one of the sectors that, since the 1920s, has experienced extremely rapid technical progress. Federal and state funds have been very important in agricultural R&D and, in contrast with the image of publicly funded R&D programs as stressing bureaucratization and centralization, publicly supported R&D in agriculture has been pluralistic and decentralized. Aviation and computers both are industries that received considerable direct R&D support by government in their early stages, and that have continued since their adolescence to receive federal monies in connection with defense and space procurement. The semiconductor industry, at least in its formative years, benefited greatly from federal procurement and R&D support.

One of the activities of the Center for Science and Technology Policy has been collecting historical case studies on the role of the federal government in the evolution of technology in a wide variety of economic sectors. In addition to those mentioned above, the study also includes pharmaceuticals, automobiles, and residential construction. As I indicated above, I suspect that the question of appropriate R&D institutions and policies ought to be explored at an industry or sectoral level, because there is so much diversity. What is appropriate - what will work, and not work - I suspect differs strikingly from sector to sector. I conjecture that understanding these differences, and their implications, is a prerequisite to understanding how we can improve the productivity of the nation's R&D systems.

5

R&D Productivity in the Semiconductor Industry: Is a Slowdown Imminent?

Richard C. Levin

The innovative record of the semiconductor industry has been one of the major success stories of the American economy in the second half of the twentieth century. In virtually every performance dimension – speed, computational capacity, memory storage capacity, compactness of equipment required for a given function – progress has been astounding. Perhaps none of the myriad statistics describing the industry's performance conveys its astonishing record so vividly as a comparison made by A. Osborne (1979). He notes that if transport technology had progressed from stagecoach to the Concorde as rapidly as electronics technology has progressed since the transistor, the Concorde would carry a half million passengers at twenty million miles per hour at a cost of less that one cent per passenger.(1)

Recently there have been expressions of concern that the pace of innovation in the semiconductor industry is likely to slacken in the near future. In part, this concern reflects a belief that the semiconductor industry will succumb to the same array of forces which have apparently reduced the pace of productivity growth across the wide spectrum of American industry. But, in considerable part, concern about the future of semiconductor innovations arises from a view that the industry is entering the mature stage of its life cycle. In this view, the semiconductor industry is headed inexorably down the road taken by the automobile and steel industries, whereupon repeated major product innovation gives way to incremental process innovation; capital requirements escalate; minimum

*The research underlying this paper was supported by grants PRA-7824096 and PRA-8019779 from the Division of Policy Research and Analysis of the National Science Foundation.

efficient scale rises more rapidly than market demand; concentration ensues; the role of small firms and new entrants as a locus of innovation diminishes drastically; and the rate of technical progress eventually declines.(2)   On the surface, there appears to be some evidence supporting this view that the industry is approaching technological maturity.   The cost of R&D and of capital equipment has been rising rapidly; there has been substantial movement toward vertical integration; entry barriers appear to be increasing; and the technological supremacy of the U.S. industry has been subject to intense competitive pressures from Japanese firms, heavily subsidized by their government.

The object of this chapter is to explore the plausibility of the view that the semiconductor industry is on the threshold of a productivity slowdown.   First, data on R&D and patents will be briefly examined to see if a slackening of innovative effort is as yet perceptible.   Second, the implications of changing technology for the structural evolution of the industry will be explored, as will the implications of structural change for the likely character and pace of future innovation. Finally, I will discuss the likely impact of a major new program of government R&D support - the Very High Speed Integrated Circuit (VHSIC) Program of the Department of Defense - and emphasize the importance of designing policies which can stimulate innovative performance without propelling the industry to an unnecessarily early maturity.

RECENT TRENDS IN SEMICONDUCTOR
RESEARCH AND DEVELOPMENT

A direct attempt to quantify the level and rate of change of the productivity of semiconductor R&D is beyond the scope of this chapter.   As noted elsewhere in this volume, the measurement of R&D productivity is an exercise fraught with peril. In an industry like semiconductors, where firms sell numerous nonhomogenous products, where each of these outputs is characterized by multiple attributes, and where good price indices for these attributes are not readily obtained, measurement of R&D productivity is a task requiring painstaking effort and a willingness to make numerous heroic assumptions.   Even the available measures of inputs to the innovative process are incomplete and not easily interpreted. In discussions with R&D managers, I have learned it is often the case that what counts as one firm's R&D is labelled routine engineering expense by another.

Quite apart from this problem of inconsistent definition, it is difficult to accurately gauge the aggregate level of innovative effort for the simple reason that most firms do not distin-

guish R&D expenditures directed exclusively toward semiconductor technology. Indeed, most semiconductor R&D is done
by firms whose reported corporate R&D includes expenditures
on computer, telecommunications, or military systems technology. Nevertheless, by pulling together data from a variety of
sources, one can begin to ascertain whether semiconductor
R&D effort has begun to decline.

   Table 5.1 presents several alternative estimates of
industry-wide R&D expenditures. Prior to 1972, the National
Science Foundation (NSF) reported relevant data only at a
very high level of aggregation, combining all R&D expenditures
of firms whose primary product was categorized by the Standard Industrial Classification as communications equipment (SIC
366), electronic components (367), or communications services
(48). In this broadly defined industry, total R&D did not
keep pace with the growth of sales; expenditures declined
slightly in real terms from 1968 to 1973 and declined more
rapidly thereafter. However, the entire decline in real R&D
spending is accounted for by a decline in government spending. Company R&D grew in real terms through 1973, keeping
pace with the growth of sales. While NSF data do not break
down total R&D by funding source for years [in the later
1970s, there is some indication that these trends - company
R&D growing in proportion to sales and government R&D declining - continued throughout the decade.](3)

   Since 1972, the NSF has reported separate data for firms
whose primary product falls within the three-digit industry
classified as electronic components. This category includes
most merchant semiconductor firms, but it excludes firms such
as American Telephone and Telegraph (ATT) and General
Telephone and Electronics (GTE) which are presumably counted
in the more highly aggregated totals just discussed. In this
more narrowly defined industry, R&D increased substantially
both in real terms and as a percentage of sales through the
mid-1970s.

   The apparently substantial increase in semiconductor R&D
is striking when compared to the pattern of total industrial
R&D expenditure in the U.S. As table 5.1 indicates, total
industrial R&D has fallen from 4.5 percent of sales in 1963 to
3.2 percent of sales in the mid-1970s. Indeed, real R&D expenditures have been essentially flat since the mid-1960s.
Interestingly, the decline is entirely attributable to the cut-
back in government-funded R&D. Privately supported R&D
has grown at approximately the same rate as the economy.

   Data compiled by the International Trade Commission
(ITC) confirm the impression of significant recent R&D growth
in the semiconductor industry. The ITC figures include estimates of the semiconductor-related R&D performed worldwide
by U.S. firms, including vertically integrated producers such
as ATT and IBM. It is interesting to compare these figures

Table 5.1. Alternative Estimates of Semiconductor R & D Expenditures

	1963	1968	1973	1977
NSF: Communications equipment and electronic components (SIC 366, 367, 48)				
Company-funded R&D ($ millions)	564	1000	1511	--
Government-funded R&D ($ millions)	1209	1538	1608	--
Total R&D ($ millions)	1773	2538	3119	3549
Company-funded R&D (% of sales)	4.2	4.0	4.0	--
Government-funded R&D (% of sales)	8.8	6.0	4.3	--
Total R&D (% of sales)	13.0	10.0	8.3	7.4
NSF: Electronic components (SIC 367)				
Company-funded R&D ($ millions)	--	--	260	--
Government-funded R&D ($ millions)	--	--	146	--
Total R&D ($ millions)	--	--	406	751
Company-funded R&D (% of sales)	--	--	3.0	--
Government-funded (% of sales)	--	--	2.3	--
Total R&D (% of sales)	--	--	5.3	7.0
NSF: Total industrial R&D				
Company-funded R&D (% of sales)	1.9	2.1	2.0	2.1
Government-funded R&D (% of sales)	2.6	1.9	1.2	1.1
Total R&D (% of sales)	4.5	4.0	3.2	3.2
			1974	1978
ITC: World wide Semiconductor R & D by U.S. firms				
Total R&D ($ millions)			330	530
Total R&D (% of sales)			15.2	14.4
ITC: Japanese Semiconductor R & D				
Total R&D ($ millions)			75	199
Total R&D (% of sales)			6.7	8.0
VLSI Program: government expenditures ($ millions)			12	33
company expenditures ($ millions)			18	50

Sources: National Science Foundation, Research and Development in Industry, (Washington: U.S. Government Printing Office, annually); International Trade Commission, Competitive Factors Influencing World Trade in Integrated Circuits, (Washington, 1979).

with ITC estimates of Japanese semiconductor R&D, which grew
at a rate far in excess of the U.S. expenditures. The very
substantial boost given to the Japanese industry by the government-sponsored VLSI (Very Large Scale Integration) program begun in 1974 is clearly indicated in table 5.1.

As further evidence of the continued rapid growth of
U.S. semiconductor industry R&D, table 5.2 presents corporate
R&D as a percentage of sales for the five leading open-market
producers of integrated circuits.(4) Of the five firms, which
together accounted for $379 million in corporate R&D expendi-
tures in 1978, only Texas Instruments has experienced a decline in the ratio of R&D to sales over the period 1973-1980.
Three of the other firms have held roughly constant, while
Intel's R&D has increased even more rapidly than its phenomenal sales growth. It should be kept in mind that these firms
experienced sales growth at average annual rates ranging from
8.4 percent to 36.5 percent over the period.

Data on semiconductor patenting activity tend to confirm
the impression conveyed by the R&D data. Patent counts are
a notably imprecise measure of R&D output, since the value of
a patent varies widely both across and within patent classes.
Nevertheless, within a single firm or a single industry the
trend in patent activity over time probably gives a reasonable
indication of whether innovative activity is increasing or declining. Comparisons made across firms are less meaningful,
since idiosyncrasies of corporate history and strategy often
lead to wide interfirm discrepancies in the propensity to patent.

Table 5.3 presents alternative measures of patenting
activity at several levels of aggregation. A report recently
issued by the Office of Technology Assessment and Forecast
(1981) reveals that for the patent classes encompassing inventions in integrated circuit structure there has been no
perceptible slackening in the rate of patents granted to U.S.
firms. There has, however, been some decrease in the number of patents granted per constant dollar of R&D expenditure. On the other hand, in the broader NSF category of
electronic components and communications equipment, patents
per dollar have increased while the rate of patenting has declined 10 percent in the decade 1967-77.

Taken overall, these figures related to semiconductor
industry activity are most reasonably interpreted as showing
no decided trend. The contrast with total U.S. patenting
activity is striking, since both the level of patenting and
patents per R&D-dollar declined 20 percent over the 1967-77
period.

The conclusion of no significant decline is reinforced by
data on patents granted to individual semiconductor firms.
The patents counted in table 5.4 include semiconductor process
and product inventions, drawn from a wider group of patent

Table 5.2. R&D as a Percentage of Sales for the
Largest Merchant Semiconductor Firms

Firm (by 1979 sales rank)	1973	1974	1975	1976	1977	1978	1979	1980
Texas Instruments	7.2	6.2	3.7	4.4	4.7	4.4	4.2	4.6
Motorola	6.6	8.1	7.5	6.8	5.9	6.0	6.2	6.5
Intel	7.0	7.8	10.6	9.2	9.9	10.3	10.1	11.3
National Semiconductor	8.8	8.8	8.8	7.6	8.2	8.7	9.4	8.2
Fairchild	9.7	9.5	11.9	9.9	9.5	9.4	-	-

Sources: Standard & Poor, Compustat data file; corporate annual reports.

Table 5.3.   Semiconductor Patenting Activity

	1967	1972	1977
Integrated Circuit Structure			
Patents granted of U.S. origin	108	145	151
Patents granted of foreign origin	9	70	99
Total patents granted	117	215	250
Patents of U.S. origin per constant million $ R&D	-	0.44	0.29
Electronic Components and Communications Equipment			
Patents granted of U.S. origin	5,546	-	5,020
Patents per constant million $ R&D	1.81	-	2.00
All Product Fields			
Patents granted of U.S. origin	51,274	-	41,452
Patents per constant million $ R&D	2.47	-	1.96

Sources: Office of Technology Assessment and Forecast, U.S. Department of
Commerce,   Patent   Profiles: Microeconomics   1,   (Washington: U.S.
Government Printing Office, February 1981); National Science Foundation,
Science Indicators, (Washington: U.S. Government Printing Office, 1980).

Table 5.4.   Patents Granted to the Largest Merchant Semiconductor Firms

Firms (by 1979 sales rank)	1972	1973	1974	1975	1976	1977	1978
Texas Instruments	58	52	61	52	69	44	43
Motorola	62	88	56	71	63	48	43
Intel	3	5	8	5	15	16	11
National Semiconductor	5	3	4	10	11	22	24
Fairchild	13	16	6	19	24	17	11
	141	164	135	157	182	147	132

Source: Office of Technology Assessment and Forecast, special computer run.

classes than used in the Patent Office report noted above. Again, it should be emphasized that each firm's intertemporal pattern is of greater significance than the variation across firms, which reflects differences in strategies regarding the protection of proprietary knowledge.

Finally, crude measures of integrated circuit technical parameters and performance do not as yet reveal a decisive slackening in the pace of technical change. The trend to miniaturization continues steadily. Minimum feature sizes shrunk at a constant rate through the 1970s to the neighborhood of two microns in 1980 for the highest-resolution production processes. The number of circuit elements per chip has roughly doubled every year, although experts expect some moderate reduction in this pace. Through the mid-1970s, memory storage capacity per chip followed a trend of doubling every year, as the successive introduction dates of the 1K, 4K, and 16K dynamic random access memory (RAM) chips were approximately two years apart. It appears, however, that the spacing between devices representing the next two fourfold improvements has increased to about three years. It is difficult to perceive a decline in the rate of technical progress from 100 percent to 60 percent per year as serious cause for alarm.

CHANGING TECHNOLOGY AND EVOLVING MARKET STRUCTURE

Although the available data do not reveal a slowdown in the generation of new technology, there are unmistakable signs of alteration in the structure of the semiconductor industry. These structural changes, which are largely the consequences of the evolving technology, fit to some degree the pattern of maturation described in the industry life cycle model of Abernathy and Utterback (1978). A strict application of the model would view these structural changes as leading inevitably to a reduced pace and altered character of technical change in the industry. In this section I will briefly describe the forces driving structural change, and then proceed in the following section to discuss the implications of structural change for the future course of semiconductor innovation.

The dominant trajectory of semiconductor technology has been toward miniaturization; progress along this trajectory requires a family of related technological advances. Scaling down individual circuit elements requires finer lines etched in the silicon substrate, which in turn requires lithographic equipment of higher resolution, silicon with fewer impurities, and more precise techniques of "doping" the silicon to achieve the desired electrical properties. Increasing the number of

functions performed on a single chip also requires advances in
the techniques of circuit design and innovations in methods of
testing and quality control. Significant progress was made
along these required dimensions in the 1970s, and most industry participants expect that miniaturization will remain the
dominant technological trajectory of the next decade.

Economically, miniaturization has been accompanied by
exponentially decreasing cost per circuit function. But miniaturization has implied significant increases in the capital
requirements of semiconductor product development and production. According to Moore (1979), the man-hour requirements of circuit design have risen more than fivefold in the
last decade. The cost of photomasking equipment has risen
dramatically. Indeed, the cost of electron-beam writers in the
coming era of very large scale integration (VLSI) is expected
to exceed the cost of optical printers used in current LSI
technology by a factor of six or more.(5) These and other
increases in capital costs underlie the economic necessity of
high-volume production. These related trends imply that
efficient-scale entry at or near the frontier of integrated circuit technology is many times more costly than it was a decade
ago.

The evidence on a new entry is consistent with the observed technologically driven increases in capital requirements
and minimum efficient scale. Among a sample of 90 semiconductor firms selected for study by Wilson, Ashton, and Egan
(1980), twenty-five entered the industry between 1951 and
1959, a rate of 2.78 new firms per year. The entry rate
spurted in the early 1960s and again from 1968 to 1971, so
that the average annual number of new firms from 1960 to 1972
was 4.69. Yet, despite rapid market growth after 1975, only
four new firms entered over the period 1973-78, a rate of 0.67
per year. This precipitous decline in the rate of entry coin-
cides with the collapse of the U.S. venture capital market; but
it seems unlikely to be wholly the consequence of reduced
capital availability. It is notable that when venture capital
resumed flowing again in 1979 a wave of new entry occurred.
But the new entrants have not aimed toward high-volume production of standardized circuits, as did a number of the successful new ventures of the middle and late 1960s. Rather,
recent entrants have sought to fill specialized niches in the
marketplace, a point that will be given due emphasis shortly.

In addition to raising the cost of new entry, miniaturization has also pushed firms in the direction of increased
vertical integration, both directly and indirectly. The direct
technological imperative for vertical integration comes from the
increasingly blurred distinction between electronic components
and systems. As more and more functions are built onto a
single chip, system design is no longer a matter of configuring
standardized components. Chip and system design have be-

come increasingly interdependent. Thus, producers of downstream electronic products have greater incentive to acquire
the capability for in-house design and production of customized
circuits. And merchant suppliers of integrated circuits have
greater incentive to design products around their innovative
circuitry.

The less direct chain of causation runs from miniaturization to vertical integration via the increased capital requirements discussed above. Despite higher entry barriers,
the semiconductor industry remains sufficiently competitive to
keep profit margins at or below the norm of U.S. manufacturing industries. In the face of rising capital costs, the ability
of smaller, independent semiconductor firms to finance growth
internally has been severely impaired. While one might have
expected greater use of external capital markets to finance
investment, the decided trend through the middle and late
1970s has been toward acquisition of semiconductor firms by
larger firms, most of them manufacturers of electronic products
or systems. Many, but not all, of the recent acquisitions have
been by foreign electronic firms, motivated by access to advanced technology and to marketing channels within the U.S.

Thus, technological forces appear to have driven the
semiconductor industry toward a market structure that is beginning to exhibit some of the attributes of maturation –
notably increases in minimum efficient scale, high entry costs,
and vertical integration. Whether these structural changes are
yet serious cause for concern is another question. The link
between a mature industry structure and a slowdown in the
rate of innovation, while well illustrated by examples in the
literature, is by no means decisively established. Moreover,
there are aspects of the semiconductor industry's recent history which strongly suggest that it has not yet reached structural maturity. Thus, for reasons to be explained in the next
section, I see little reason to conclude that a slowdown in
innovative performance is imminent. Nevertheless, there are
policy decisions on the horizon which will be influential in de-
terming whether the forces driving continued technological
dynamism are to be strengthened relative to the forces driving
the industry toward maturity and diminished innovativeness.

THE IMPLICATIONS OF STRUCTURAL CHANGE
FOR INNOVATIVE PERFORMANCE

In stylized models of the industry life cycle, technological
competition eventually produces a relatively small number of
surviving firms – typically integrated both vertically and
across a full line of related products, enjoying economies of
scope and scale, and protected by substantial barriers to

entry. In such an environment, radical product innovation gives way to incremental product change and refinements in process technology. Oligopolistic interdependence and comfortable profit margins dampen the vigor of technological competition and productivity gains proceed at a modest pace.

This characterization may apply, in very broad outline, to some "mature" U.S. industries: for example, automobiles and major electrical appliances such as washers, dryers, and refrigerators. But despite rising entry costs, and the growing importance of scale and vertical integration, the semiconductor industry does not yet resemble the typical "mature" industry. First of all, while there have been some clear winners and losers in technological competition, market concentration has not yet begun to rise significantly. The top four producers of semiconductors had 33 percent of worldwide sales in 1971, 32 percent in 1975, and 30 percent in 1979.(6) Moreover, there has been substantial turnover among the market leaders. Only one (Texas Instruments) of the top five U.S. producers of transistors in 1955 is among the top five producers of integrated circuits today. Five of the top ten integrated circuit producers in 1975 were not among the top ten semiconductor firms in 1965, and four of these firms were established after 1960. Today's semiconductors industry contains not three or four major full-line producers with substantial technological sophistication, but perhaps 15 or 20 firms worldwide with the capability for significant innovation and market penetration across a range of technologies and applications.

Even if the technology race in the semiconductor industry had produced a smaller number of survivors and a more concentrated industrial structure, it is not obvious that the rate of innovation would slacken as a consequence. The link between market structure and innovation is not so simple. Technological competition influences market structure by producing successful firms which expand and failures which contract. Market structure in turn influences the incentives to innovate. The claim of life cycle theorists that oligopoly channels innovative effort in conservative directions is plausible; but so is the Schumpeterian argument that concentration enhances the predictability of the economic environment and thus promotes investment in technologically risky, long-term projects. To disentangle the likely impact of market structure on innovation, it is essential to isolate the independent forces which jointly influence both realized market structure and innovative performance. These forces include the underlying demand for the industry's products, the inherent scientific and technological opportunities confronting the industry, and the ease by which the returns from innovation can be appropriated by an innovator.

When one reflects upon the demand, opportunity, and appropriability conditions facing the semiconductor industry, it is evident that the industry bears little resemblance to those industries which are paradigmatic of the mature stage of the life cycle. In contrast to the demand for automobiles and household appliances, which is almost exclusively a demand for replacements, demand for electronic components is continually augmented by the opening of new markets and introduction of new applications. There is little on the horizon to suggest that the demand for integrated circuit technology in consumer, industrial, and military applications will cease to grow at rates well in excess of the overall growth rate of economic activity. Of equal importance is the apparent fact that technological opportunity in microelectronics remains abundant. Reinforcing the data presented above on R&D activity is the consensus view of experts in semiconductor technology that there are no fundamental physical limitations to the further pursuit of min-iaturization over the next decade. There are eventual thermal constraints on the density of circuitry contained on a chip, which will ultimately necessitate a transition to superconductor technology for some applications. But most experts agree that further substantial increases in circuit density are forseeable with the use of advanced lithographic techniques presently under development.(7)

The demand and opportunity conditions facing the indus-try thus strongly indicate that a slowdown in the rate of innovation would be unlikely even if the industry were highly concentrated. That it is not is in a large measure a conse-quence of the severe constraints on appropriability that have characterized the semiconductor industry since its infancy. As is well-know, technology diffuses rapidly across semiconductor firms, for a variety of reasons. Important aspects of propri-etary technology, such as circuit design, are not patentable under existing law. Even where patents are available, they offer little protection because cross-infringement is so wide-spread as to render most patents unenforceable in practice. Reverse engineering has been relatively simple, and interfirm employee mobility in Silicon Valley is legendary. Limited ap-propriability has not yet exerted a significant dampening influence on the rate of innovation, probably because demand growth has been so rapid and opportunity so abundant. With rapidly growing demand, a few months of lead time with a new product have been sufficient to insure adequate reward to innovative activity. When the market for microelectronics approaches saturation (an event still in the distant future), the ease of imitation will no doubt accelerate tendencies toward a reduced pace of innovation.

Thus, despite substantial recent changes in the structure of the semiconductor industry, the market is not yet highly concentrated, and demand, opportunity, and appropriability conditions appear to favor continued rapid technological progress. The fact remains, however, that the cost of undertaking R&D at or near the frontier of semiconductor technology has escalated rapidly, and the cost of entry into full scale integrated circuit production has grown substantially. Although I have argued that the overall pace of innovation will not slacken dramatically, these structural changes nevertheless have implications for the character of semiconductor R&D and its distribution across firms. In particular, it is likely that small firms and new entrants will play a rather different role in the advance of semiconductor technology.

In the past, small firms and new entrants have had substantial impact on the direction of mainstream technology. New firms, such as Fairchild in the late 1950s and Intel and Mostek a decade later, achieved major process and product innovations and jumped rapidly to positions of both technological and market leadership in pivotal, high-volume product areas. Today, it is much more difficult to imagine a grass-roots entrant moving directly to a position of market leadership in semiconductor logic or memory devices. The cumulative R&D experience of the large established firms, the complexity of the technology, and the cost of assembling the required personnel and equipment now appear as formidable barriers to a frontal assault on a major market via product or process innovation.

It is therefore likely the next several generations of general purpose memory and logic devices will be introduced and imitated by larger established firms. Such devices are the types most likely to realize the remaining latent economies of miniaturization. Innovation (and even imitation) along this trajectory will be costly, and an expectation of high volume production will be necessary to justify the investment. Innovation along this trajectory will also require related advances in lithography, materials quality, circuit design, packaging, software, and testing. Only large established firms are likely to have the human, organizational, and financial resources necessary to pursue simultaneously these related developments.

Nevertheless, certain areas of opportunity remain open to smaller firms and new entrants. Many of these opportunities arise as a consequence of demand for innovative applications by small and medium scale downstream producers lacking independent semiconductor fabrication capability. While many downstream users have made innovative use of standardized circuits produced in large volume by major merchant semiconductor firms, other have increased the demand for custom designed circuits for specialized applications. Virtually all of the new semiconductor firms established in the past two years have specialized in one or more of the related areas of custom circuit design, computer aided design (CAD), custom fabrication, and custom software. Semicustom design and fabrication, where silicon wafers are processed for various applications in

identical fashions up to a final step of one of two custom designed masks, has also been a growing area of interest.(8)
     Smaller firms may prove to have a comparative and per-
haps absolute advantage in custom and semicustom work.
Many custom demands can be served cost-effectively by technology that is not at the very frontier of the miniaturization
trajectory. Consequently, custom design and fabrication hous-
es do not require investment in human capital and in state-
of-the-art process technology on the scale of a large merchant
semiconductor firm. At the same time, there is doubtless
substantial idiosyncratic skill developed by designers who
specialize in custom services, which may compensate for higher
unit fabrication costs. Many industry experts believe that the
most fruitful applications of CAD tools will be in the design of
custom or semiconductor circuits well within the miniaturization
frontier. Nevertheless, innovations in CAD, custom design,
and fabrication may have a high payoff in productivity en-
hancement in downstream industries, even if they do not have
the effect of increasing function density or improving circuit
performance parameters.

PROMOTING INNOVATION IN THE SEMICONDUCTOR INDUSTRY: THE VHSIC PROGRAM

Amidst public concern for the future of the semiconductor
industry, the U.S. government has embarked upon a major
program of R&D support for military applications of advanced
technology. The impetus for initiating the VHSIC (Very High
Speed Integrated Circuit) program was quite independent of
civilian concerns about the industry's future or its standing
relative to Japanese competition. Rather, planning for the
program began in 1978 immediately after military intelligence
reports revealed that the U.S. advantage in the electronics
embodied in fielded weapons systems had been significantly
eroded. The principal objective of the VHSIC program is to
establish the capability for fielding weapons systems utilizing
high speed integrated circuits of submicron feature-size by the
end of the decade. Technically, one of the program's central
goals is defined as an increase of two orders of magnitude in a
critical parameter which is the product of speed (clock rate)
and circuit density (gates per cm^2).
     Technologically, the goals of the VHSIC program are
highly compatible with the continued pursuit of miniaturization
in the commercial segment of the semiconductor business. The
military has certain specialized needs, such as the ability of
circuitry to perform under extreme conditions of temperature
and radiation. But much R&D funded by VHSIC, such as
support for advanced lithographic techniques to facilitate real-

ization of submicron feature sizes and support for improved CAD, software, and testing methods, should have significant spillovers to commercial application. In turn, the independent pursuit of similar technological objectives for commercial purposes should facilitate the achievements of VHSIC goals. Indeed, the planned Department of Defense expenditure of approximately $200 million over seven years is far less than industry will spend on its own; but there is an emerging consensus that the added stimulus provided by VHSIC funds will move forward the realization of submicron circuits by two or three years.(9)

When the VHSIC program was first announced, it was enthusiastically received by most major suppliers of military electronics systems; but several leading merchant semiconductor firms expressed serious reservations, and some chose to abstain from bidding on VHSIC contracts. A major concern was that the VHSIC program would divert scarce R&D resources, especially critical personnel, from pursuit of commercial objectives. It was feared that VHSIC would handicap U.S. firms in competition with the Japanese for leadership in VLSI technology. These fears seem to have been misplaced, as industry participants have come to recognize the substantial complementarity between VHSIC and commercial VLSI objectives. On the other hand, it would be a mistake to view the VHSIC as a direct response to the Japanese government's support of the semiconductor industry. While it now appears that VHSIC will provide an indirect boost to U.S. firms in technological competition with the Japanese, merchant semiconductor firms still seek policy assistance more directly related to meeting the Japanese challenge. The legislative program of the Semiconductor Industry Association (1981) has three major components: tax incentives for R&D expenditures; access to the Japanese domestic market via relaxation of tariffs and controls on direct investment; and support for engineering education.

Early critics of VHSIC also questioned the program's emphasis on supporting large scale vertically integrated research efforts. The program as envisioned involved vertically integrated firms or teams of firms, and each proposal was expected to tackle a range of issues from circuit fabrication technology and process equipment to insertion of circuits into weapons systems. Critics feared that the emphasis on large firms and vertically integrated teams would hasten concentration of the semiconductor industry and reinforce the trend toward vertical integration, allegedly threatening the vitality of a highly competitive and dynamic merchant semiconductor industry. Congress initially delayed funding until it received assurances that the program would not have an anticompetitive impact on the industry.

As it has developed, the major portion of R&D support will be allocated to vertically integrated contractor teams responsible for developing the technology necessary at all levels to utilize submicron integrated circuits in operational weapons systems. Initial nine-month Phase O contracts were awarded to nine such teams in 1980, and in May 1981 six of the teams were selected as contractors for Phase I of the programs, which will extend into 1983. It is unlikely that confining VHSIC support to six teams (five of which involve merchant semiconductor firms; one contract was won by IBM) will increase concentration in the industry, especially since several nonparticipating firms will be pursuing VLSI technology with private resources on a significant scale. But the initial Congressional worries about market concentration did encourage the Department of Defense to develop a program design that preserved niches of opportunity for small, non-integrated firms as well as university research laboratories.

Paralleling the mainstream Phase I and II efforts will be a series of much smaller contracts to be awarded on a continuing basis throughout the duration of the program. These smaller Phase III contracts will focus on narrow technical problems, where significant contributions complementary to the Phase I and II objectives can be expected from firms outside the mainstream program. It is expected that Phase III contracts will be concentrated in areas such as lithography, CAD, software, and testing. In concept, Phase III represents a reasonable safeguard against the somewhat remote potential that the VHSIC program will unduly accelerate the industry toward maturity and stagnation. In any case, it appears to be an example of organizational design well suited to maximizing technical advance. On the one hand, major support will be given to not one, but several, large-scale vertically integrated efforts. On the other hand, substantial funds (one-third of the total budget) will be reserved for smaller scale projects complementary to the program's overall objectives. In principle, such an organizational design can be utilized to generate innovation from both large and small firms in the areas where each has a comparative advantage.

Given this rather creative institutional design, the results of the first round of Phase III contract awards are somewhat discouraging. The first Phase III contracts were let several months before due date for Phase I proposals; consequently, virtually half (77 of 157) of the proposals submitted came from the large firms involved in the mainstream Phase O program. Evidently, Phase O winners saw in Phase III an opportunity to impress the DoD with good work prior to the major funding decisions on Phase I proposals. Of the 157 proposals received, only four came from qualified small businesses and only eight came from nonintegrated semiconductor firms. Only one of these twelve was among 53 funded proposals, while 24 contracts were awarded to Phase O participants. Somewhat more encouraging was the award of 11 Phase III contracts to five different universities.

It is evident that if the VHSIC program is to benefit from innovative ideas from a variety of sources, more attention must be paid to encouraging the submission of proposals from small and nonintegrated firms. Managers of the program are aware of this problem, and they have taken steps to drastically simplify the format of the second-round Phase III request-for-proposals. Indeed, there is a growing recognition throughout the DoD that opportunities for small firm participation in R&D support programs have been diminished by the escalating complexity of the contracting process. In a very promising development, the DoD initiated in April 1981 a new Defense Small Business Advanced Technology Program. Proposals are solicited by a lucid 23 page document, a striking contrast to the 100 pages of boilerplate contained in the first round request for VHSIC Phase III proposals. If the VHSIC program follows this lead, prospects will be enhanced for the preservation of a dynamically competitive semiconductor industry structure with variegated sources of innovation.

NOTES

1. This striking comparison was called to my attention by Rosenberg and Steinmueller (1980).

2. The view that industry evolution follows a typical life cycle pattern, with the mature stage exhibiting the features indicated in the text, has been widely discussed in the literature on technical change and industrial organization. For a full articulation of the life cycle model, see Abernathy and Utterback (1978), Abernathy (1978), and Utterback (1979).

3. In the case of ATT, which accounts for a substantial fraction of the R&D in this industry category, private funded R&D grew slowly but steadily as a percentage of sales over the period 1973-80, while government-funded R&D performed by ATT declined precipitously in real terms and as a percentage of sales. (Source: ATT annual reports, 1973-80).

4. According to estimates made by Integrated Circuit Engineering (1980), IBM's production of integrated circuits for internal use exceeds the production level of each of the leading merchant semiconductor firms listed in table 5.2. ICE's estimate of ATT's captive production places it just below the sixth-ranked merchant semiconductor firms, Signetics, and above such significant merchant producers as Mostek, AMD, and RCA.

5. This figure is documented by Robinson (1980).

6. These concentration ratios are derived from sales estimates reported by Dataquest (1980). Captive production by IBM, ATT, and other firms which do not sell semiconductors in the open market are excluded.

7. For two representative statements of this view see Keyes (1977) and Noyce (1977).

8. For an interesting discussion of recent developments in custom and semicustom design and fabrication, see Integrated Circuit Engineering (1981).

9. For an interesting and detailed survey of progress made during the first nine months of VHSIC funding, see Aviation Week and Space Technology, February 16, 1981, pp. 48-85.

REFERENCES

Abernathy, W.J. 1978. The Productivity Dilemma. Baltimore: Johns Hopkins University Press.

Abernathy, W.J. and J.M. Utterback. "Patterns of Industrial Innovation." Technology Review, June/July 1978, pp. 41-47.

Aviation Week and Space Technology. "Technical Survey: Very High Speed Integrated Circuits." February 16, 1981, pp. 48-85.

Dataquest. 1980. Semiconductor Industry Services, Appendix B. Cupertino, California: Dataquest.

Integrated Circuit Engineering. 1980. Status 1980: A Report on the Integrated Circuit Industry. Scottsdale, Arizona: ICE.

_____. 1981. Status 1981: A Report on the Integrated Circuit Industry. Scottsdale, Arizona: ICE.

Keyes, R.W. "Physical Limits in Semiconductor Electronics." Science, March 18, 1977, pp. 1230-35.

Moore, G.E. "VLSI: Some Fundamental Challenges." IEEE Spectrum, April 1979, pp. 30-47.

National Science Foundation. Research and Development in Industry. Washington: U.S. Government Printing Office, annually.

_____. 1980. Science Indicators. Washington: U.S. Government Printing Office.

Noyce, R.N. "Large Scale Integration: What is Yet to Come?" Science, March 18, 1977, pp. 1102-06.

Office of Technology Assessment and Forecast, U.S. Department of Commerce. Patent Profiles: Microelectronics I. Washington: U.S. Government Printing Office, February 1981.

Osborne, A. 1979. Running Wild: The Next Industrial Revolution. Berkeley, California: Osborne/McGraw-Hill.

Robinson, A.L. "Giant Corporations From Tiny Chips Grow." Science, May 2, 1980, pp. 480-84.

Rosenberg, N. and W.E. Steinmueller. 1980. "The Economic Implications of the VLSI Revolution." Working paper, Stanford University.

Semiconductor Industry Association. The International Mircoelectronic Challenge. Cupertino, California: Semiconductor Industry Association, May 1981.

U.S. International Trade Commission. Competitive Factors Influencing World Trade in Integrated Circuits. Washington: USITC, November 1979.

Utterback, J.M. 1979. "The Dynamics of Product and Process Innovation in Industry," in C.T. Hill and J.M. Utterback, ed., Technological Innovation for a Dynamic Economy. New York: Pergamon Press.

Wilson, R.W., P.K. Ashton, and T.P. Egan. 1980. Innovation, Competition and Government Policy in the Semiconductor Industry. Lexington, Mass.: Lexington Books.

6

The Competitive Decline in U.S. Innovation: The Management Factor

William J. Abernathy

The productivity of R&D in our economy depends on the operation of our industrial system. When we examine its recent performance, and look carefully at several cases that involve technical change and innovation, we realize that management structure and approach can be critical to our understanding of R&D productivity.

About fifteen years ago, something went wrong in our economy. Something went very wrong. Consider the many indicators that point to the same problem.

Statistics on national R&D expenditures (see figure 6.1), show that the peak years of U.S. supremacy in R&D investment as a percent of GNP were around 1963 to 1965. The crossover point - when the Russians exceeded U.S. R&D levels - was about 1968. The Russians are now spending a great deal more than we are on R&D, as Figure 6.1 shows. Also, other nations are now approaching our expenditure ratio. Of course, there are problems with defining R&D, and one might question whether it really matters that much anyway. But there's more.

---

*This paper draws on two previous papers in its conception: William J. Abernathy and Richard S. Rosenbloom "The Institutional Climate for Innovation in Industry: The Role of Management Attitudes and Practices," Policy Outlook: Science Technology and the Issues of the Eighties, AAAS Report to the National Science Foundation, Washington, D.C., 1981, pp. 35-78; and Robert Hayes and William J. Abernathy, "Managing Our Way to Economic Decline," Harvard Business Review, July/August, 1980, pp. 67-77.

National expenditures for performance of R&D's as a percent of Gross National
Product (GNP) by country, 1961-76

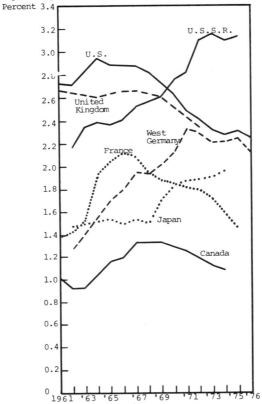

Fig. 6.1.   Investments in technology.

[1]Gross expenditures for performance of R&D including associated capital expenditures (except for the United States and
the U.S.S.R. where total capital expenditure data are not
available)

Note: Estimates are shown for 1974, 1975 and 1976.   United
         Kingdom figures for 1968-69 are shown as 1968, 1969-70
         as 1969 and 1972-73 as 1972.

Source: National Science Foundation.   Science Indicators 1976
           Washington, D.C.: Government Printing Office, 1977,
           p. 5.

Another set of data (see figure 6.2) concerns changes in types of innovation. The sample size of 277 isn't very large, but it was enough to trace changes in the incidence of radical innovation in three periods. This figure suggests that radical innovation has declined significantly over the period from 1953 to 1973. Conversely, shifts in technology have gone up. According to this data, it seems as if the U.S. is relying more on existing technologies (by shifting technology applications) while relying less on radical innovations. This shift apparently had its origins in the 1950s. The sample size may be contested, and there are problems in defining innovation; it may be argued, again, that these innovation data don't mean very much.

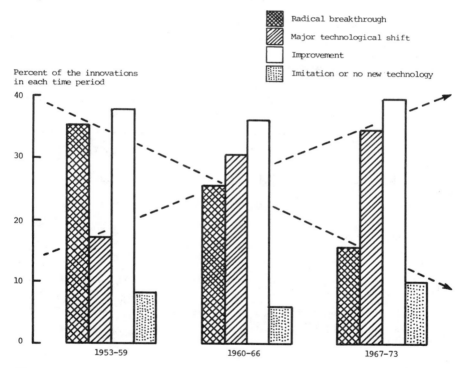

Fig. 6.2. Estimated radicalness of major U.S. innovations, 1953–73.

Note: Based on sample of 277 U.S. innovations

Source: National Science Foundation, Science Indicators 1976 (Washington, D.C.: Government Printing Office, 1977, p. 122).

As a third indicator, we can look at national productivity data (see table 6.1) by comparing the periods 1960-1973 and 1973-1977. The United States had a 3 percent rate of productivity growth in the first period and a 2.2 percent in the second - whereas Germany had 5.5 and 5.6 percent rates in the same periods and Japan had 10.2 and 7.7 percent rates. The United States is certainly ahead of the United Kingdom in productivity, but there are few other countries behind us; in fact, we were roughly on a par with Italy according to these statistics.

Table 6.1. Changes in labor productivity

Growth in Labor Productivity Since 1960
(United States and Abroad)

	Average annual percent change	
	Manufacturing 1960-1978	All Industries 1960-1976
United States	2.8%	1.7%
United Kingdom	2.9	2.2
Canada	4.0	2.1
Germany	5.4	4.2
France	5.5	4.3
Italy	5.9	4.9
Belgium	6.9*	---
Netherlands	6.9*	---
Sweden	5.2	---
Japan	8.2	7.5

*1960-1977.

Source: Council on Wage and Price Stability, "Report on Productivity" (Washington, D.C.: Executive Office of the President July 1979).

What do productivity figures mean? They are merely another indicator - piled on top of a lot of other indicators - that says the United States is falling behind in innovation and in productivity.

Another trend shows that the United States holds second place in machine-tool production. West Germany now holds the lead in capital goods and machine tool production (as shown in table 6.2). The machine tool industry is more significant than other industries because sales can be seen as an index of process innovations in the producing country. In other words, new machine tool output is stimulated by process innovations; the fact that West Germany passed the United States in absolute terms reflects on innovative performance. When machine tool sales are taken as a fraction of gross national product, the situation is worse: the United States is likely to rank behind Italy.

Yet another indicator of declining competitiveness arises from data on the balance of patents (see figure 6.3). Whereas

Patents granted to U.S. nationals by selected foreign countries and to foreign nationals by the United States, 1966-75

U.S. patent balance with selected countries, 1966-75

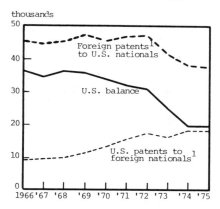

[1]Including only Canada, West Germany, Japan, the United Kingdom, U.S.S.R., Belgium, Denmark, Ireland, Luxembourg, and the Netherlands. Data for France and Italy are not reliable for use in this indicator.

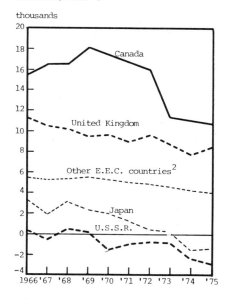

[2]Other European Economic Community (E.E.C.) countries include Belgium, Denmark, Ireland, Luxembourg, and the Netherlands.

Fig. 6.3.   Trends in Patenting.

SOURCE: National Science Foundation, Science Indicators 1976 (Washington, D.C.: Government Printing Office, 1977, p. 21).

Table 6.2. The Decline of U.S. Technological Capabilities

World Machine Tool Production and Trade – 1976 Estimated
(Values in U.S. $ Millions)

COUNTRY (Top 12)	PRODUCTION TOTAL	CUTTING	FORMING	TRADE EXPORT	IMPORT
1. West Germany (FGR)	2,393.2	1,479.6	913.6	1,636.5	234.4
2. United States	2,030.0	1,440.0	590.0	530.0	335.0
3. Soviet Union*	1,915.2	1,372.6	542.6	222.1	600.0
4. Japan	1,078.6	806.4	272.2	338.2	92.2
5. East Germany (GDR)*	776.1***	604.5***	171.6***	620.0**	200.0
6. Italy	708.6	456.4	252.2	348.3	144.1
7. Great Britain	634.7	466.3	168.4	318.3	252.6
8. France	627.2	451.6	175.6	271.8	342.9
9. Switzerland	523.3	444.8**	78.5**	419.6	69.1
10. Poland*	499.3	449.8	49.5	159.0	480.0
11. Czechoslovakia*	355.7	251.1	104.6	207.8	98.3
12. China	325.0**	250.0**	75.0**	5.0**	60.0
WORLD TOTAL	13,141.6	9,339.5	3,802.1	5,753.7	4,200.4

*Controlled currency at official conversion rate; real equivalent hard to determine.
**Rough estimate from fragmentary data
***Target

SOURCE: The Machine Tool Trades Association. Some Basic Facts: The British Machine Tool Industry
(Lewes Sussex, England: W. E. Baxter Ltd., 1978).

the U.S. had a superior balance relative to other nations a few years ago, this is no longer the case. One may also argue that these data are also not very significant. But when it is all added up, the several different indicators amount to imperfect evidence on many fronts that says that something is wrong - the United States has some sort of a national problem which is very difficult to identify.

Two examples can help to clarify the nature and possible origins of the problem. The first is the consumer electronics industry as a whole; the second concerns automobiles.

CONSUMER ELECTRONICS

In 1955, the U.S. output of consumer electronics was about $1.5 billion.(1) Japan's was about $700 million. The United States clearly dominated the consumer electronics industry in this period. It had the highest volume production of any country in the world, while Japan's industry was small and feeble.

Now the situation is reversed. The Japanese have well over twice our output and more importantly, the United States has not innovated significantly over this period, at least not until the recent videodisc developments.

Home video recording, the development of the Trinitron Television tube, the transistor radio, and small television sets are all dominated by the Japanese. The United States has been impotent as far as this industry is concerned.

To examine the consumer electronics case in more detail, the clock must be turned back. In 1955, there was a very small internal market for television sets in Japan of roughly $30 million. But a boom was underway in the 50s, and the Japanese electronics industry had a hard time keeping up with the internal demand. That didn't slow them down, for they quickly managed to place heavy emphasis on developing the pocket transistor radio for international markets.

Although there had been earlier U.S. development of such radios, it was not successful. U.S. producers were frustrated by the lack of progress in the miniaturizing of components. The Japanese were successful, and the transistor radio was used to achieve market entry into the United States. Until that point, there had been very little Japanese electronics in this country. Even by 1960 there were no serious Japanese inroads into the U.S. market for television sets.

It is common knowledge that many market-research surveys at this time showed there was no market for small television sets. Market research showed a preference of the market for 19-inch and larger sets. But Sony apparently didn't appreciate market research. They introduced a tiny, transistorized set called the "Tummy T.V." Their ad showed a jolly rotund man lying in bed with a little television set propped up on his tummy. From this base, massive inroads were made into the bottom end of the market. This "bottom-end" entry mode was to become the Japanese strategy in many industries.

The next challenge was the video recorder - another example of the United States providing the basic innovation. (Previously, the United States invented the transistor, but the Japanese made the pocket-sized transistor radio). Ampex, in about 1956, developed the video recorder. It was a major innovation. Demand was intense and Japanese broadcasting stations, among many others, owned several sets. Apparently foot traffic to the stations was heavy in those days, as Japanese engineers went to view the video recorder and explore its design.

The original set included a large console and two racks of equipment. It cost about $50,000. Ampex designated it as a "quad" machine because of the format of the tape; Ampex also experimented with a helical format, which promised to lead to a cheaper product that used less tape. (The "helical" designation signifies the way the signal is recorded by the tape head.) Ampex decided that helical designs offered a lower-quality approach unsuitable for the commercial industry to which they were selling recorders. (In the late 1950s, RCA did, however, take out patents on the helical format, as did Telefunken and Toshiba.) When Sony considered the potential of the video recorder in the 1950s, a long-run target was set for their engineers to reduce the cost by a hundredfold - that is, to reduce the cost to one hundreth of the $50,000 Ampex design - and to get tape consumption down. The goal was to make the video recorder a viable consumer product. Their efforts were focused on the helical design.

Few companies have set such challenging goals. A one hundredfold cost reduction for a product as complex as the Ampex machine presents a seemingly impossible challenge for a commercial organization. Sony not only set such a goal - they set it in a serious tone. Of course, the setting of a goal doesn't mean the goal will be realized. For Sony there were a lot of roadblocks and hurdles in the way of creating a consumer version of a video recorder. As shown in table 6.3, Sony introduced its first model by 1962. It was one-twentieth the size and a fifth the price of the original Ampex machine. It sold for approximately $10,000. In 1965, they introduced another model that used half-inch tape and could be produced for one percent of the original cost.

By 1965, Sony had realized many aspects of their market goal, but they still didn't have a functional consumer product. In 1974, Sony finally came out with the Betamax. The difference between the original Ampex and Sony's new machine was

Table 6.3. Milestones in VTR Product Development.

MARKET	MODEL	COMPANY	DATE OF COMMERCIAL INTRODUCTION	TAPE WIDTH*	TAPE UTILIZATION (sq. ft./hour)	PRICE (in constant 1967 $)
BROADCAST	VR-1000	AMPEX	1956	2"	747	$ 60,000
PROFESSIONAL	VR-1500	AMPEX	1962	2"	375	$ 12,000
INDUSTRIAL	PV-100	SONY	1962	2"	212	$ 13,000
INDUSTRIAL/PROFESSIONAL	EL-3400	PHILIPS	1964	1"	188	$ 3,500
INDUSTRIAL/PROFESSIONAL	CV-2000	SONY	1965	1/2"	90	$ 600
INDUSTRIAL/PROFESSIONAL	N-1500	PHILIPS	1972	1/2"	70	$ 1,150
INDUSTRIAL/PROFESSIONAL	U-Matic	SONY	1972	3/4"	70	$ 1,100
CONSUMER	Betamax	SONY	1975	1/2"	20	850
CONSUMER	VHS	JVC	1976	1/2"	16	790
CONSUMER	VR2020	PHILIPS	1980	1/2"	6	520

*From 1972 onward, all models used cassettes instead of open reels and all used high-energy tape.

Source: W.J. Abernathy and R.S. Rosenbloom "The Institutional Climate for Innovation in Industry: The Role of Management Attitudes and Practices" Policy Outlook: Science, Technology and the Issues of the Eighties. AAAS Report to the National Science Foundation, Washington, DC, 1980. p. 53.

phenomenal. A big part of this was getting tape consumption down so that the consumer could afford the tape. Shortly thereafter, in 1976, Japan-Victor, the corporate daughter of Matsushita, brought out another video recorder of substantial quality. Sony is a firm with very long-term objectives carried through with a great deal of vigor.

Taking the consumer electronics business as a whole, a conclusion that U.S. management has played a very meager role in the industry's progress cannot be avoided. What are the major patterns associated with these past 25 years of development in consumer electronics? One characteristic is that no one single firm was responsible for all the work on any single innovation. A lot of the innovation was adopted and a lot of it was borrowed from other firms; but there isn't the original Ampex kind of innovation, in which a single firm contributes all the advances for an entire product and then brings it to market. Borrowing from other parties and cross-licensing seems to be the more common pattern. The Japanese firms became specialists in consumer electronics. None of the surviving U.S. firms, with perhaps the exception of RCA, chose to become a consumer electronics specialist.

There were 150 television set manufacturers in the United States in 1955. The industry shake-out, however, came very rapidly. Consolidation has so continued to the point that today there are almost no American producers in the continental United States. The Japanese producers play a more substantial role in U.S. production than the original U.S. producers. The original U.S. producers have largely moved offshore to Mexico, Hong Kong, and other lower-cost manufacturing sites.

The traditional explanations from economic theory offer little insight about the failure of the American consumer electronics industry. From what we might call a "Federal Trade Commission" point of view, the structural conditions for innovation were certainly present: there was not a concentrated oligopoly nor any apparent barriers to entry or to innovation. Why, then, did the American firms neglect innovation as a competitive strategy? There certainly seems to have been few barriers to innovative competition among the 150 television set manufacturers in the 1955 era. The cause must be sought elsewhere.

One potentially important explanation of competitive performance among American firms is that management turned their backs on the industry. Under a common assumption that the market was mature and that consumer electronics wasn't very interesting, attention was focused on computers, semiconductors, products in the other sectors; few - if any - firms took a long-term, developmental point of view in their approach to the consumer electronics industry.

To summarize, there were no deficiencies in the United States technological capabilities, nor were there structural barriers in the industry to preclude innovation. There were no direct capital deficiencies to stand in the way, nor was inflation a problem in the 1950s and early 1960s. The important conclusion, which the consumer electronics industry seems to suggest as one case example, is that the problem of deficient competitive performance really originates as a "management of innovation" problem. Management turned its back on this industry segment, or for other reasons decided to take short-run points of view and not innovate competitively.

Consumer electronics is one example. Another example stems from recent work on the automobile industry. (2)

AUTOMOBILE INDUSTRY PRODUCTIVITY PROBLEMS

One contemporary view of the automobile industry productivity problem rests on recent testimony by certain elements of the administration (i.e., the Council of Economic Advisers during the Carter term) regarding foreign trade legislation. In much of this testimony, it was held that there were essentially no productivity differences between the United States and Japan. The real problem, according to this testimony, is the wage differential. Productivity rates among the two nations were claimed to be roughly equivalent. The cost of employing an American worker is roughly $18 per hour, versus the Japanese $9 per hour. If the average car requires 100 labor hours in production, this implies a labor wage differential of $900 per car. Netting out delivery and tariff charges, the landed-cost advantage is between $200 to $400 per car in favor of Japanese producers.

In almost direct contradiction to the administration's conclusions, however, recent data suggest an enormous productivity gap. According to this new information, the Japanese require roughly half the man-hours per car that American producers require. They seem to make a car in 50 hours, whereas American producers require closer to 100 hours per car. Although differences in vertical integration must be accounted for, the problem is a very significant one in terms of absolute productivity differences. At the same time, the difference is not the result of capital investment deficiencies. It is a "management of people" problem. Even in comparing comparably automated plants, man-hours per car seem to be much lower in Japan. This amounts to another $800-$900 per car. This data suggest that, all told, the Japanese enjoy a $1,200-$1,600 landed-cost advantage - a very large gap!

This means the quick solution that might be realized if only an increase in capital investment were required is not achievable. In a financially oriented business community, it is easy to think that all one has to do is get the investment criteria right and the problem will go away. This isn't valid. Massive productivity differences seem to stem from differences in work force involvement. It seems that it's a people problem rather than a hardware or capital problem.

The solution depends upon a new kind of management-union-and-work force relationship. It means getting rid of the adversarial relationship with labor; it means putting together a task-oriented, competitively oriented, work force. Agnelli, the chief executive of Fiat, made the point in the company's most recent annual report that it is a purely academic exercise to speak of competition under free trade conditions when there are such large differences in attitudes between Italian and Japanese work forces.

There is also a big difference in corporate work force relations between the United States and Japan. A long tradition of adversarial relationships guide collective bargaining in the United States. In the resulting "effort bargain," wages have been traded for the "hands and legs" of labor - but not its commitment. Traditionally, American workers have not seen themselves as part of the competitive picture in international rivalry. The Japanese worker has.

All is not black. A host of changes are occurring in the auto industry. General Motors is trying twelve or more different approaches to improve its relationship with labor. Ford is also trying some new approaches. For the first time, they put a stop button on their assembly line. Now workers can be responsible for quality; they couldn't be responsible for quality when the line could not be stopped and defective products went right by.

Although a lot of change in going on, there has been a long period of neglect of productivity issues in U.S. industry. This allowed a small country like Japan, that had in 1963 lower productivity in the automobile industry, to take over and gain a double advantage in both labor rates and productivity rates. It's going to take a long time to recover from a two-to-one productivity advantage.

From a broad perspective, the reason U.S. firms have gotten into trouble is because management has essentially turned its back on many avenues of competition. Labor was eliminated as a competitive variable when the industry wide bargaining process was adopted. This gave all firms the same labor conditions; thus, the firms no longer needed to care about labor, since added costs would be passed on uniformly by all competitors. Management essentially turned its back on many productivity-enhancing, innovative opportunities.

THE ORIGINS OF THE PROBLEM

What are the lessons from these cases? How do they extend to
the general case? To answer these questions it is important to
step back and consider the origins of competitive problems in
U.S. industry in general.

There are several causes. One has been excessive mer-
ger activity - firms getting into businesses they know nothing
about in a market or technological sense. Interesting work
has been done recently by William Fruhan at the Harvard Business School on the real benefits, from the stockholders' perspective, of mergers and financial acquisitions.(3) There is a
growing body of evidence that, although the intent of such
mergers is often to develop a larger sale base, to create stock
value through merged assets, or to gain the liquid surplus of
declining companies, the end result most frequently does not
benefit the stockholder, much less the consumer. The "unrelated" or "pure conglomerate" mergers among Fortune 500
companies (see table 6.4) seem to have offered poorer performance than the all-industry average. In "multicompanies,"
where acquisitions were semi-related, the return on capital was
9.7 percent; in conglomerates the return on capital was 8.8
percent; whereas the industry average was 10.2. When measured by sales growth, the merged companies still fall behind.

Table 6.4.   Performance of Multicompanies

FIVE-YEAR AVERAGE

	RETURN ON CAPITAL	SALES GROWTH
MULTICOMPANIES (25)	9.7%	9.7
CONGLOMERATES (44)	8.8%	10.3
ALL INDUSTRY AVERAGE	10.2%	12.9

SOURCE: Forbes, January 8, 1979.

One of the reasons for low levels of innovative activity is
traceable to the diversification trend. Management thought the
quickest way to achieve short-run gains was through financial
manipulation. The time delays are shorter and the risks of

growth are lower when development occurs through "conglo-merization" and diversification. But the result is that firms get into unrelated businesses in which top management doesn't know enough about markets or technology to make creative investments. Investment decisions in such firms are increas-ingly made on the basis of financial analyses, which means looking at past performance rather than looking forward to the future.

No matter how sophisticated the approach in financial analysis, it is difficult to do anything but "look where the boat has been" and to reward people on that basis. This emphasis on diversification represents but one area where management has gone astray.

A second source of decline in U.S. competitive advantage seems to stem from the increasing transfer of technology abroad. Professor Raymond Vernon of Harvard has developed some interesting data which outline the problem of increasing technology transfer out of the U.S.(4) He studied the dif-fusion of an innovation from the time it is introduced in the United States by a multinational to the (later) time it is in-troduced abroad. In 1945, 10 percent of the products in his sample were introduced abroad within one year of U.S. intro-duction, and eight percent were introduced within the next two to three years. Therefore, some 82 percent were not diffused abroad during the first three years following incep-tion. By 1975, however, 25 percent of the innovations were diffused abroad within the first year of introduction in the United States; 16.2 percent were diffused abroad within the next two years. Thus, a total of roughly 40 percent of the innovations developed in the United States are diffused by multinational corporations within three years, and only 60 percent are retained.

This means the United States as a nation no longer has as much time as it once did to derive benefits from its inno-vations. They are no longer a national property. The whole idea of the international product life cycle is brought into question by these data. It is not clear that the United States can maintain a proprietary national position in an innovation or that the whole concept of "targeting" makes much sense. Can a target be set on a sunrise industry and a sunset industry allowed to falter when there is very little faith that the sun-rise industry can be sustained? The whole matter deserves much more consideration than it has received.

Another major area of change since the 1950s has been the origins and experience base of management personnel. (See figure 6.4.) Based on data from a management consulting firm, it appears that the origins of chief executive officers (CEOs) for the Fortune 500 companies have gone through loops and swirls since the 1950 period. Whereas technologists – generally production people, engineers, and scientists - were

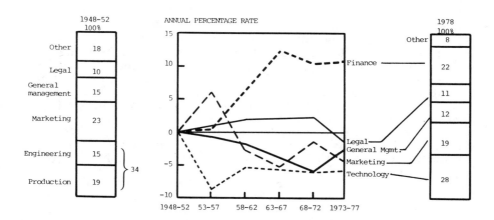

Fig. 6.4.   Change in professional origins of U.S. corporate presidents. Top 100 companies, base line years 1948-52.

SOURCE: Golightly & Company International, 1978.

by far the most frequent source of CEOs in the early fifties, there has since been a significant increase in the number of CEOs who come from financial and legal posts.

This swing in the experience paths of CEOs has more influence than is apparent from the numbers alone. The "road to the top" is sought by many of the brightest young people, who are acutely aware of trends. If financial expertise provides new access to the top for some, then there are a lot more people who will want to get on the bandwagon and become "financial jocks." In fact, that is what happened in the late sixties and early seventies. All of a sudden a wave of "get on the bandwagon and become a financial jock" took over.

The use of small profit centers and various financial control devices has often overwhelmed the personal contact that is found in innovative organizations like Hewlett-Packard, 3-M, and Bell Labs. In these companies, the executive officers seem acquainted with all the company's technological projects if not with all the individuals involved. As president of Hewlett-Packard, David Packard had a practice of participating in the design-review meetings of all the projects of the company. That sort of personal contact between the CEO and the engineers who are doing the project is something that is reportedly much more prevalent in Japan than it is here.

Among this list of changing management characteristics that have affected U.S. competition, the most visible change is the growing list of financial-based management tools. Many of these categorize the operating divisions of firms according to what is essentially their stage of development. One category might describe a situation in which a product line has a high market share and a high growth rate in the industry. Here, there is typically a high demand for cash. If a division is growing, it needs money. Conversely, if there is a low growth rate and a high market share, then, according to this model, there will tend to be a large positive cash flow.

These techniques become tools for describing subordinate businesses in a way that helps to place them into categories. The typical breakdown might include "stars," which are the high growth rate, high market share businesses; "cash cows," which are the low growth rate, high market share divisions; "dogs," in which everything is low; and "question marks." These terms have become a pervasive language in the business community.

Different kinds of management are recommended for each category of business. Over the life cycle, the type of management, the role of management, managerial compensation, organizational structure, planning time, planning content, content of the management reporting systems, and corporate departmental emphasis, all change. The business starts out in the embryonic state or the creative state, in which an entrepreneurial emphasis is very important. It ends up in a mature state where the conditions needed for mass production are important. But the problem is that, once a business is categorized this way, its fate is determined by the category. If the classification is as a mature industry, how can this designation be changed if conditions change? This is particularly a problem if decisions are dominated by an abstract formulative financial management system.

I learned of one company, a company specializing in medical textiles, that had been designated a cash cow by its parent company. Even in the face of new business opportunities yielding 30 percent return on investment after tax, the division could not get itself reclassified. Their competitive task was rigidly constrained to that of being drained of assets. Even though its management had tried to get an altered status with corporate management, they could not arouse enough attention. The answer remained "you're a textile business and you remain a dog." Maybe what happened in consumer electronics is that management decided the whole consumer electronics area was a dog and assigned appropriate management.

That is only an hypothesis, but it is clear there was no emphasis on innovation as a competitive strategy for growth.

Finally, there is the issue of market research. Too often management relies on specific market research confirmation in setting goals for innovative programs. This has been a mistake in case after case. Formal market research, which tends to do an excellent job on existing products, fails on innovative products. In one instance during the early 1970s, an electronics firm conducted formal market research on the potential for pocket calculators. The conclusion was that there was no potential. Not surprisingly, those surveyed, having never experienced the new technology, had little appreciation for its potential. Similarly, the initial market forecasts for computers in the years immediately following World War II suggested that ten large main frame machines would be enough to solve the world's computing problems. It is not that good market analyses can't be done; it is more that survey research in this area of new technology is treacherous. The problem is how to perceive the way that the market is connected with the technology. This does not seem to be often done very well through formal surveys.

To summarize, there is little question that the United States has experienced a significant decline in its competitive performance. The problem, while often blamed on inflation, an inadequate rate of capital investment, and so forth, may in large part be a failure in management. From the evidence considered here, the consequences illustrate a failure of management insight and financial pressures. The causes of these management problems are not management ineptitude; rather, they are seen to originate in new methods of management which favor a control process which is formal and financially based. As a solution, management itself must take action. This is not a problem which can be solved by sweeping government policy changes. The answer lies squarely in the lap of today's business leaders.

NOTES

1. The case of innovation in the consumer electronics industry is more completely discussed in W.J. Abernathy and R.S. Rosenbloom "The Institutional Climate for Innovation in Industry" Policy Outlook, AAAS Report to the National Science Foundation, 1981.

2. National Academy of Engineering, "The Competitive Status of the U.S. Automobile Industry," by Kim Clark. A draft version of the Automotive Panel, in preparation.

3. Fruhan, William E., Financial Strategies: Studies in the Creation, Transfer and Destruction of Shareholder Value (Homewood Il: Richard D. Irwin), 1979.

4. Raymond Vernon, "The Product Cycle in a New International Environment," Oxford Bulletin of Economics and Statistics, Vol. 41, No. 4, 1979, pp. 225-267.

7
Strategic Planning and R&D Productivity in a Decade of Change
D. Bruce Merrifield

Industry today is critically concerned with finding the best strategies for effective capital investment. During inflationary periods of the sort we are now experiencing, this concern is particularly acute for capital-intensive, low-asset-turnover industries.

Measures of R&D productivity tend to focus on outputs in the form of new products, processes, and services. But a more realistic measure of R&D productivity requires a hard look at its effects both on maintaining the viability of current investments and also on the directions to which it points for new investments. Indeed, from the standpoint of top corporate management, the interrelationships between investment in R&D and the ultimate direction of future corporate investments may well be the most fundamental determinant of R&D productivity.

Allocation of resources to industrial technology must be seen as a business, not a technical, decision. Moreover, investments in technology must compete with other demands for always limited resources; therefore, to be effective, this function must be carefully integrated into a corporate strategic plan. Statistics tend to be poor. Perhaps one of 20 significant programs that start out in the laboratory ever produces a positive cash flow. Moreover, the greatest improvement in these statistics can come from "working smarter rather than harder."

In effect, "working smarter" translates to better strategic planning, coupled with better integration of all the operating elements into the strategic plan. An order of magnitude improvement in R&D productivity is conceivable in this context. The first step in realizing such a significant increase in productivity is a semiquantification of the forces which are currently shaping the environment.

The decade of the 80s will almost certainly be a major watershed period in which many well-known companies disappear or are restructured, and other new companies emerge as industrial leaders. In fact, the growth, and in many cases survival, of many American businesses in the 80s will be primarily determined by two interacting factors. One of these is economic and the other involves technology. The economic factor involves an adverse synergism between current U.S. tax laws and chronically high rates of inflation, which together are causing many American companies to liquidate their fixed assets, often without conscious awareness that they are doing so.

The technology-related factor arises from a worldwide explosion in the sciences that in the last 30 years has generated some 90 percent of the current knowledge in physics, chemistry, engineering and the biological sciences. The direct result of this explosion of technology is that much of the capital now invested in this country is invested in obsolescent products and processes. It is important to understand both the risks and unparalleled opportunities that are associated with these two factors.

THE EFFECT OF INFLATION

The asset-destroying effect of inflation shows up clearly if we consider a numerical example:

Return on Equity (ROE) -	Dividends Paid Out -	Rate of Inflation =	"Real Retained Earnings"
15% -	7%* -	10% =	-2%

The equation shows that a company reporting a solid 15 percent return on equity (ROE) is actually <u>eroding</u> its assets in "real" terms when inflation is running at 10 percent per year, and when the company is paying out the U.S. average of about 47 percent of its earnings in dividends, and has minimal debt (2/1 equity to debt ratio). Many capital-intensive businesses (steel, automobiles, tires, shoes, etc.) do not report even a 15 percent ROE and are liquidating their assets at 5-15 percent per year.

*Represents about 47 percent of reported earnings - the average payout for U.S. companies.

In principle, a company can reduce its dividend payout and/or leverage its assets (1/1 equity to debt ratio), but these strategies affect the market price and increase vulnerability to takeover. The net effect, therefore, is that recent tax laws - which have not adjusted for inflation - have provided rates of depreciation that are insufficient to reproduce the original assets at the end of their "useful life." Compounding the problem is that new technology is rendering assets obsolete long before their "useful life" is realized. The adverse synergism of these factors (inflation, tax laws, new technology) is threatening the survival of many well-know companies.

For example, a $10 million investment in a manufacturing plant with a "useful life" of 20 years until recently could be recovered in depreciation allowances over that period. But at 10 percent inflation, the same plant would cost $80 million to replace. Moreover, the $70 million difference would not have been reserved. Instead, the difference would have appeared on the balance sheet as false profits on which 46 percent taxes and 40-50 percent dividends would have been paid out.

The adverse political-economic climate that now exists for fixed-asset-intensive operations calls for a new set of business guidelines.

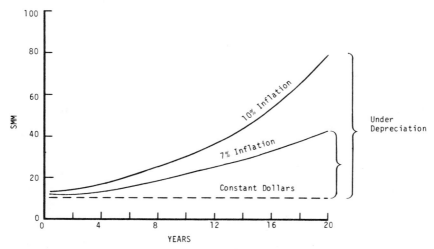

Fig. 7.1.   Under-Depreciation in an Inflationary Regime.

1. Given a policy of 2/1 equity-to-debt and 40-50 percent dividend payout, any operation that has more than 60-70 cents of depreciating assets per dollar of sales cannot produce real retained earnings in a period averaging 10 percent inflation, and should be harvested or divested.

2. The resulting cash flow should be allocated to either:

   a) those businesses which have appreciating assets and/or are "indexed to inflation" such as oil and gas, timber, land, financial and other services, etc., or

   b) to low capital-intensive, high growth, strongly proprietary (patented) products or processes.

These may be unattractive options for an established company, however, since they necessitate radical changes in operating strategy. The anxiety involved in entering an unfamiliar business is often multiplied by a reluctance to concede that the existing business may not somehow survive, let alone grow. Good acquisitions carry a heavy premium in goodwill, and internally generated new ventures have had some notable failures. The dilemma is real.

The dilemma is also understandable, and there may be a logical explanation for it. In the early 1920, the Soviet economist N.D. Kondratieff first identified a 50-year recession-boom cycle or "long wave" that, at the time, had persisted for 150 years and that seemed to characterize the capitalist economies. (To suggest that capitalism tends toward an oscillating pattern of collapse and resurgence rather than to a secular decline was, to say the least, a rather unfashionable opinion for Kondratieff's time and place; he was promptly dispatched to a Siberian salt mine in 1930).

Recently, Jay Forrester of the Massachusetts Institute of Technology has rediscovered the same cycle. His data base comes from a "System-Dynamics National model" built up in some detail from 15 major industrial sectors. Forrester identifies four phases in the 50-year cycle. The first is a 15-year recession period; the second is a 20-year massive reinvestment period; the third is a 10-year continued "overbuilding" period; and the fourth is a 5-10-year period of economic turbulence leading into the next recession. This is illustrated in figure 7.2.

It appears unlikely, however, that a 1929-type recession will now or ever again recur. Instead, we are seeing a major watershed period in which many well-known companies may not survive in their present form. Simultaneously, we are seeing the emergence of new companies in new technologies at a rate that has never before occurred.

Going back to 1929, the beginning of Phase I of the last Kondratieff-Forrester Cycle, the economy was characterized by zero or negative GNP growth; high rates of inflation (more than 10 percent per year); a low ROI in capital-intensive sectors; declining profits; increased debt; tightening credit;

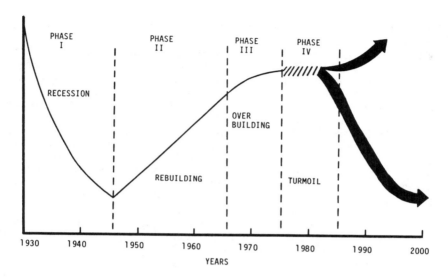

Fig. 7.2.   Kondratieff long wave.

declining capital investments; high interest rates; and, perhaps most importantly, overcapacity relative to worldwide
demand.

    In the political and social areas, unemployment was ris-
ing, radical political elements were becoming more active, crime
and terrorism were rising, and the labor pool was characterized by obsolescent skills and resistance to movement into new
technologies.   The focus of management was no longer on
production, but primarily on legal and financial aspects of
business; R&D budgets were both declining in constant dollars
and were focused more tightly to short-term product optimi-
zation.   Major new innovations tended to be discouraged or
rejected.   Management tended to be anxious and very conservative.   Plant facilities and equipment tended to have reached
the limit of productivity for that state-of-the-art, and justified
little additional investment.

    As the cumulative effects of overcapacity, cutback in
investment, and conservative management were felt, the world
economies slid into a recession that required about 15 years to
depreciate existing facilities and equipment and to reestablish
an excess demand over supply.   However, at the end of Phase
I GNP growth was still low.   Inflation also was low; debt had
been reduced (by bankruptcy); interest rates had declined;

and the economy was poised for a massive reinvestment fueled by a pool of new technology that had been accumulating for 30 years. This new technology resulted in much higher productivity and decreasing inflation even though credit was easing and the money supply was rapidly increasing. A 20-year rebuilding program then started (schools, homes and highways, as well as new plant facilities and equipment). The labor pool rapidly shifted into the newly developing business areas with company-sponsored training programs, and political turmoil subsided. Management was refocused on technology and production as the 30-year pool of accumulated technology was now being rapidly exploited.

At the end of Phase II, supply and demand were again in rough balance, but the momentum was tremendous. Credit was easy, inflation low, profits and ROI high, and new technology again was being rejected in favor of doing more of what was already successful. Management was bullish, expanding beyond domestic markets into remaining niche growth areas and focusing more on optimizing the current technology.

This began Phase III, in which overcapacity was built and cash flow was ploughed almost compulsively back into the existing businesses. The risk seemed low, labor was skilled, and alternative investments seemed less certain. By the end of this period, however, ROI's had declined, inflation had begun to rise, interest rates were higher, debt was rising again; but capital investments continued. By the end of Phase III, warning signals were beginning to emerge. The four-year business cycles became deeper, unemployment began to be a problem, and political activists emerged again. The scene is now set for the beginning of another 50-year cycle. In fact, 1981 is the 52nd year of Kondratieff's 54-year cycle.

Indeed, the new cycle may already have started. Fixed-asset-intensive companies in the United States have been liquidating themselves in real terms for seven of the last nine years. And the key factor in their liquidation is their inability to increase productivity in obsolescent facilities. The open-hearth furnace can no longer compete with the basic oxygen furnace, let alone with the new Swedish plasma technology. And soon, graphite-reinforced plastics, which are stronger than steel, lighter than aluminum, and don't corrode, will further erode the metal markets. In fact, the new "engineering plastics" will capture specialty markets now using steel, aluminum, zinc, and copper, as an explosion in materials science provides an increasing array of options superior in cost performance for many applications.

But, while steel, automobiles, and other commodity systems involving obsolescent facilities decline, the 30-year pool of underutilized technology that has built up (and represents 90 percent of knowledge in the sciences) will continue to spawn an enormous array of new businesses - the IBMs and

the Xeroxs of the next decade. Explosive growth in electronics, communications, lifelong adult education, engineering
plastics, specialty chemicals, biogenetics, energy and energy
systems, etc., will more than pick up the slack. These new
businesses will not only grow rapidly but will also have higher
asset-turnover ratios, making them much less vulnerable to
inflation. These technologies also offer proprietary opportunities in niche markets that carry high margins and much higher returns on equity. As a result, many current mass markets will fragment into niche or specialty segments, and the
management of the future will be the management of continual
change.

It appears unlikely that the Untied States will experience
another 1929-like collapse now or in the future. Instead, a
major disproportionation or watershed will occur during the
next decade, and those companies doing effective strategic
planning will thrive while others fail, are restructured, or are
taken over. Once this traumatic readjustment period is over,
the United States may be launched into one of the most stimu-
lating periods in history. A major characteristic of this regime
will likely be a continuous evolution of new (and obsolescence
of older) technologies within 5-10 year time-frames - thus
bringing to an end the 50-year cyclic buildup-and-collapse
syndrome.

If the measure of R&D productivity can be defined in
terms of the value that results from resources invested in its
function, then the productivity of R&D can be expected to rise
rapidly in an environment which will be generating unparalleled
opportunities for investment in high-growth proprietary products, processes, and services. The key to increased productivity will be in the use of a combination of functions:

- One of these will be a continuous intelligence, search,
  and analysis function which sifts the worldwide explosion
  in technology for both threats to and opportunities for
  current business interests.
- A second will be a licensing, acquisition, and joint venture function capable of exploiting the search function.
- The third is a highly competent internal technical function, which can further develop, translate, and innovate
  around or within an increasing spectrum of technologies.

In the end, it may be not only possible but probable that
R&D productivity and the quality of life of most developed
countries could see an exponential improvement over the next
decade as these forces of change unfold. The United States in
particular, with the unparalleled depth, breadth, and strength
of its industrial infrastructure, could be the major beneficiary.
Moreover, those organizations that develop a strategic plan
consistent with change, and that integrate their operating

functions into that plan, will likely thrive. The technology function and its productivity must be seen as an integral part of such a systems approach.

8

Commercial Evaluation of Research and Development

Lowell Steele

The commercial evaluation of research and development is only one of several perspectives required to attempt to measure the productivity of R&D. One important dimension is associated with evaluating the efficiency of the operation of the R&D establishment, including an appraisal of the caliber of the people involved in the technical work.

A second dimension is associated with improvements in what one might term the "tools of research," i.e., the techniques, analytical procedures, measurement instruments, information processing capabilities, etc., that enable the scientist to perform his work with greater rapidity or, in some cases, to undertake experiments or tests which otherwise would be impossible.

A third dimension involves the choice of the programs to which the R&D organization will devote its energy. This, in turn, subdivides into two categories: one is concerned with the technical promise of the work being undertaken; a second involves the "fit" of the potential outputs with the sponsoring enterprise. This chapter will focus on this third dimension.

In undertaking a commercial evaluation of research and development, it is important to realize that R&D is not an end in itself. The purpose of research and development is to create the basis for technological innovation. That entire process, of which research and development is only the initiating step, is a lengthy and complex one; however, the process is more likely to be successful if the research and development organization produces outputs that have some reasonable fit with the capabilities and plans of the sponsoring organization.

TYPES OF R&D OUTPUT

It is important to realize that the types of R&D outputs that should be included in any evaluation go well beyond the popular perception of the contributions of research and development to the industrial enterprise. The economist, for example, tends to associate the outputs of R&D with opportunities to reduce factor costs. Economic theory is not well equipped to deal with the process of product innovation where cost is not the primary outcome of the innovation, but rather a new level of value for the customer.

One can distinguish at least eight different types of R&D outputs that may emerge in varying proportions from a particular research and development organization, depending on its charter, mission, and the specific obligations imposed on it by management. The most obvious one is inventions leading to new products. This is the one most visible in the popular literature, but it cannot be ordered up on demand, and, depending on the situation in the sponsoring organization, it may not even be what is most needed.

Of greater importance to most companies is evolutionary improvement in the state-of-the-art that leads to continuing - if possibly undramatic - improvements in the performance attributes of the enterprise's products, reductions in its costs, or improvements in user convenience. The latter may be as important to the growth of the total market as improvement in attributes itself.

The third output, and one frequently overlooked, is improved capability for manufacture. This could include advances in processes for the fabrication of parts, automation of assembly and material handling, or computer aids to manage the flow of information associated with the production process.

A fourth category is improved capability for information flow and communication. This includes information systems for managing the business; data communication networks; the development of high-level languages and software tools to improve the development of information technology itself; and office automation and all the related capabilities that have so much effect on industrial productivity. Except for those companies directly involved in the communications and information systems businesses, these contributions may be the most frequently overlooked output of R&D.

The fifth output is improved tools for performing R&D itself. Increased knowledge, improved capability for measurement, computer aids for data acquisition and reduction all can have a significant effect not only on the R&D organization itself, but on downstream capabilities in engineering design, development, and test. The capability to analyze product attributes, to simulate performance, and to design by computer all have an enormous impact on productivity and on speed and flexibility of response.

The sixth output of R&D, also frequently overlooked, is the development of application information for customers. Industrial customers typically need detailed, quantified, rigorously developed information about product attributes in specific operating regimes in order to make intelligent choices in the selection of materials or components and to incorporate them in the design in a valid manner.

A seventh output of R&D involves trouble-shooting for products or processes that are not performing satisfactorily, and where the first-level efforts at diagnosis and repair have not been successful. When greater sophistication in measurement analysis and conception are required, the R&D organization is frequently called in.

The final output involves the development of the necessary health, environmental, and safety information to meet growing regulatory requirements and societal demands.

The extent to which a particular research and development organization provides outputs in each of these categories will vary depending on the nature of its mission, the wishes and needs of the sponsoring organization, the stage of development of particular technical programs, and the immediate requirements of operating components.

MEASUREMENT CRITERIA

The various attempts at quantifying the value of the research output inevitably focus on only one, or at most a few, of the outputs included in this list. Furthermore, these attempts imply a degree of rigor that is not yet possible in most measurements. This situation is not unlike that which general management faces in much of its measurement activities, where it finds that it must blend a combination of judgment and quantification in making its evaluation.

The management measurement criteria that are applied, either quantitatively or qualitatively, in evaluating R&D can be posed in terms of three questions:

(1) Does the R&D organization appear to perceive and address the full range technologies relevant to the enterprise? Industrial executives think of the R&D organization as their insurance, protecting them from nasty surprises by providing continuing opportunities for future growth. They inevitably compare what they know of their own research and development activities and what they are told by the R&D managers with what they are told by their own operating management, what they read and hear about opportunities and problems

being experienced by others in industry, and what they see competitors doing.

(2) Does research and development management reflect the appropriate priorities in allocating resources? This balancing of priorities should recognize the current corporate mission and the strategy being pursued by the corporation, the charter assigned to the R&D organization to provide inputs to the company, and the current business situation (including not only profit prospects, but the specific needs and opportunities of the various operating entities). Industrial managers expect the R&D manager to maintain a long-term perspective because that is his mission, a mission that must be finely tuned to reflect awareness of, and appropriate responsiveness to, operating realities and constraints.

(3) Does R&D management achieve the appropriate balance of responsiveness and autonomy? The R&D organization cannot ignore immediate problems and current operating needs; but, by the same token, if it operates in a totally responsive mode it is not performing its mission of protecting the long-range future of the enterprise.

THE EARLY STAGE: AN EVALUATION SYSTEM

As this discussion has indicated, the typical research and development organization provides a wide variety of outputs in varying proportions at different times. In these circumstances, it is unlikely that any single evaluation process is going to be effective. What is needed is a sequential evaluation with each step being attuned to the nature of the activity at that stage. In the early stages of R&D one faces a situation in which there are many program candidates that have to be put through some sort of screen. The list will possibly be hundreds; it will certainly involve many dozens of programs. In most cases, the spectrum of program opportunities represents a very diverse span of subject matter. Consequently, there will be difficulty in having ready at hand the kind of expertise needed to make detailed critical evaluations. In the early stages of research and development there is typically limited information with which to work. A significant degree of uncertainty simply cannot be resolved, no matter how much information one obtains at early stages - there is much that is unknowable. Intrinsically, the R&D manager is forced to make judgments on grossly inadequate information.

On the other hand, the situation that exists at this early stage is one in which the resources commitment on individual programs is not large. Probably the most important resource involved is people, not money.

What kind of evaluation system works best in this situation? First, one wants an evaluation system which enables management to focus its attention on the controversial programs. In an ongoing laboratory situation, there is already broad consensus as to the importance and promise of most of the programs. Consequently, the evaluation system should force management to focus its attention on those programs about which there are questions.

A second attribute of a successful evaluation system is that it will match the rigor of analysis applied with the quality of data and the time constraints that management must meet. If one doesn't have much data, if many programs must be evaluated, if the resource commitment for any one of them is not large, or if large elements of uncertainty are unresolvable, then it is not cost-effective to insist on an elaborate evaluation process with detailed quantification before making program decisions.

A third attribute of an effective evaluation system is that it must be one primarily by line management. There are two reasons for adopting this approach. The first is that it is desirable for line management itself to engage in the evaluation exercise in order to experience the intellectual discipline that is involved in evaluating programs. The second is that if a separate professional evaluation group is established, its output will inevitably be regarded as a target for line management to try to destroy. If line managers make the evaluation in the first place, they are accountable for trying to achieve the results of their efforts.

A fourth attribute is that the evaluation process should help focus attention on areas of disagreement and help to clarify the sources of the disagreement. If the process partitions the evaluation task into pieces, such that one can find out where there is agreement and where there is disagreement, then one can be constructive in resolving the disagreement. Otherwise, the evaluation exercise may turn into a shouting match.

The final attribute is the desirability of introducing commercial considerations early into the evaluation process. If one has a competent technical organization (and most technical organizations will meet at least minimum requirements) the problem of technical validity is rarely important as the dominant criterion for making program selection choices. The principal challenge is to identify which out of a series of program proposals represent the ones that have the largest potential commercial impact on the enterprise.

EVALUATING THE POTENTIAL IMPACT OF R&D

The problem the R&D manager faces is that of evaluating potential impact among a variety of programs in some consistent manner where adequate data for doing so are frequently lacking, and where an extensive data-gathering process is not warranted. The determination of relative program value requires answering two questions. First, what difference will it make if this program is successful? Second, how likely is this program to succeed, given the nature of the technical problem and the skills and capability of the organization? We have identified four dimensions in evaluating potential impact: market size, rate of growth, opportunity for market penetration, and sensitivity to technology.

With respect to market size, obviously one would prefer to work on projects that aim at a large market rather than a small one. One way of evaluating market size (keeping in mind that at this stage extensive market research is not warranted, or even possible) is to draw analogies to present businesses in the company. In many cases it is not necessary to work by analogy because the program is, in fact, focused on existing businesses. In other cases the R&D manager might be able to say that this project, if successful, could lead to a market opportunity approximately equal in size to that of a specific existing business in the company - thus, by analogy, approximating likely market size.

Rate of growth is an important consideration because more rapidly growing markets are inherently more attractive than slowly growing, or declining ones. Frequently, in the early phases, one is limited to evaluations of the rate of growth of a particular segment of industry rather than the precise market for a new product. Again, where external market research data are not available it is sometimes possible to establish ranges for rates of growth by making comparisons with already existing company businesses. In general, one would prefer to work on projects aimed at markets that are growing more rapidly than the average for the company.

Opportunity for market penetration is an important and sometimes overlooked consideration. This penetration will be influenced by the competitive situation - how many competitors are there, and how well entrenched are they? Obviously, it is also influenced by the skills and resources of the company that can be brought to bear on this particular market opportunity, including managerial skills and attitudes about change. Is the market likely to be dominated by a single major competitor? Or is the competitive structure widely dispersed with no clear evidence of leadership? In some cases it may be that one's own company is the likely dominant factor in the market.

In none of these dimensions - market size, rate of growth, or extent of penetration - does technology loom as a critical factor. The final consideration is the sensitivity of a given market to technological advance. Some markets are much more technology-driven than others. Improvements in product attributes - efficiency, size, life, maintainability, cost, etc. - largely determine success for some classes of products. For others, style, price, advertising, broad distribution, after-sales service, etc. are key factors.

RANKING R&D PROGRAMS

Various techniques can be used to establish an approximate order of value for programs using these criteria. The limited accuracy of data precludes elaborate schemes. One easily applied system is to establish an approximate dollar value for the size of the potential market, using relatively large increments as a step function, and then to use the other criteria (rate of growth, likely level of penetration and sensitivity to technology) as a series of discounts to reduce the value of the market opportunity. Since one is dealing with a broad dispersion of programs with a wide range of values, a logarithmic scale may be useful. A range of market sizes can be designated in half-decade increments, going from 30 million to 100 million to 300 million to 1 billion. The discounts can also be set in a similar decreasing half-decade scale going from 1 to 0.3 to 0.01, etc. One should expect the scale to be exceedingly spread out because the intent is to identify the few attractive opportunities from the large number of those with more limited attraction.

The answer to the second question - "What is our likelihood of success?" - again involves a series of four criteria: (a) degree of difficulty of the technical problem; (b) competitive status of the particular approach proposed; (c) fit with the resources of the organization; and (d) likelihood of being able to effect the transition from lab to market.

Technical problems can vary in difficulty from those that have defied mankind since the beginning of time to those that almost certainly can be solved if resources are but applied to the task.

The evaluation of the competitive status of the particular approach requires knowledge of the status and promise of programs being pursued elsewhere. Is it a situation in which another organization already has an exceedingly promising approach with substantial momentum built up? Is it one in which the proposed approach is at least as good as those being pursued by others? Or does the organization already have substantial momentum on what appears to be an exceedingly promising approach?

The fit of the resources of the organization with the requirements of the program has an important bearing on the likelihood of this particular organization's success with the program. Are skills and facilities of the type that would be necessary already in place, or at least readily attainable? Or are they quite foreign to the traditional work of the laboratory, leading one to expect some considerable difficulty in obtaining such resources and employing them productively? The more a program departs from the traditions of the organization, the greater the risk that the program will not be successful. When managers are not used to a technology, they feel less competent in judging people; their projections of the time and resources required to achieve stated goals are less certain; and their self-confidence in persisting despite difficulties is more likely to be shaken.

The likelihood of being able to effect a transition of the technical results, if successful, into commercial application is perhaps the most important criterion of all. Does an operating component already exist in the firm that would be able to take on the new technology? Does that component have the requisite technical competence to undertake the transition? Is its financial position such that it would be able to divert resources to undertaking such a development? Perhaps most important - how willing is the management to undertake change? Or does the technology face the problem of having no likely home in the company?

The evaluation of program value in the sense just described can be represented in a matrix (see figure 8.1) where impact is shown on one dimension and likelihood of success shown on the other. This evaluation procedure is appropriate to use in connection with what could be termed "focused research programs" in which the commercial potential is beginning to be recognized. This system is inappropriate for the evaluation of basic research programs where technical promise itself, together with the caliber of the people undertaking the work, are the principal criteria for evaluating programs.

In addition to this screen for evaluating impact and likelihood of achieving success, it is necessary to consider programs in terms of their contribution to the basic charter and mission of the organization, and the fundamental priorities that have been established for its work. This framework must be worked out in a dialogue with senior management of the company. Clearly, certain types of work must be undertaken and completed before resources can be diverted to work of lower priority. Typically, the highest priority will go to activities to protect present businesses of the company, to insure that they stay healthy, or that businesses in trouble are returned to a state of health. Only after these needs have been satisfied can resources be devoted to pursuit of additional opportunities or to probing for breakthroughs that could lead to

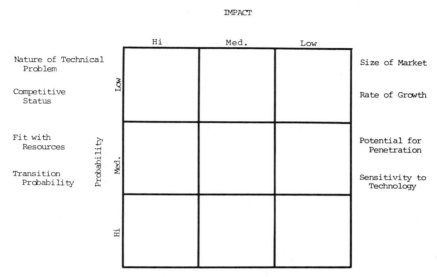

Fig. 8.1.   Screen for Evaluating R&D Programs.

new programs in the future.   This spectrum can be thought of
as an urgency screen, moving from must do, to should do, to
might do.

An evaluation system of this sort imposes a mental discipline on the management to insure that it is identifying the
most appropriate questions on which to focus attention.   In
addressing these questions management can be sensitized to
the nature of the management task ahead.   Thus, if a program
is initiated that presents the company with a severe transition
problem, management is alerted that this problem must receive
the highest priority of its attention.

EVALUATION AT THE LATER STAGES

The problem evaluation procedure should, of necessity, become
more rigorous, detailed and demanding as programs move closer to the stage of commercialization.   One is now looking at
many fewer programs - perhaps only a dozen.   The range of
subject matter involved in these programs has become much
more limited.   Furthermore, these programs are reaching the
stage at which a large resource commitment will be required.
This resource commitment will tie up a significant fraction of

the dollars and manpower of the organization. By this stage of development, the areas of uncertainty have become relatively clear. The requirements that must be met in resolving them have been specified. By that some token, however, a much more substantial information base has been established. Perhaps most important of all, operating management has begun to be involved in the process.

The specifications for a program evaluation system at this stage are quite different. The evaluation should be led by operating management rather than R&D management. Tentative product attributes and prices need to be established to form the basis for financial and market projections. Market size and characteristics need to be established. Cost projections need to be made. Capacity and capital requirements need to be established. These are all areas in which operating management quite properly regard themselves as the experts. An evaluation prepared by R&D management would be regarded as questionable not only because they are not considered to be experts in these areas, but also because they are likely to be seen as biased in favor of the new technology. Since it is operating management that will have to live with the results, it is important for them to be responsible for generating the numbers.

Program evaluation at this stage is an iterative process, frequently done quarterly, or possibly on a more frequent basis. It will continue to examine the question of product attributes, cost projections, payback periods, and market projections.

A MULTIDIMENSIONAL PROCESS

It is apparent that the commercial evaluation of R&D must be a multidimensional process, with different evaluation systems being applied at different stages of the process and being performed by different people. One of the most troubling facets of the task of the total evaluation of R&D is that, as noted at the beginning, R&D is but the first step in the process of innovation and all of those other steps must be performed successfully by quite different people if the R&D output is ultimately to achieve the desired impact on the company. Operating executives are well aware of these complexities. They would, in fact, be deeply suspicious of a proposed evaluation scheme that reduced all this complexity to a single evaluative number indicating performance.

Additional effort is clearly needed to measure the impact of R&D outputs compared with costs. Of equal importance is better understanding of the requirements for the management system within which the planning, conduct, and measurement

of R&D occur. This system must ensure that: all of the needed perspectives are present at each stage in the process; the
decision process generates a common understanding of the
imponderables; and balance between opportunity and cost is
kept under continuing, but sympathetic scrutiny.

In the absence of such a supportive management system,
an arsenal of sophisticated measurement tools is unlikely to be
of much value.

9

Research and Development Productivity: From Good to Better

Arthur G. Anderson

INTRODUCTION

When one thinks of Research and Development, it is common to expect fundamental, profound, or revolutionary change brought about by keen insight, brilliant tenacity, and often elements of luck. Thus, the subject of R&D productivity must certainly concern itself with such dramatic changes in productivity. Any experienced R&D manager can think of many cases in which the consequences of a new idea, a new leader, or a new tool has been a dramatic increase in productivity. Significant changes do occur, and they are usually worth the effort involved in bringing them about.

But there is another way to approach the question of improving R&D productivity. This approach begins from the position of an organization whose productivity is already good and looks to incremental improvements that move the organization consistently to an even better productivity position. This approach requires a belief that improvement is always possible and that, even when achieving the goal seems doubtful, a constant striving for improvement remains imperative if the organization is to grow in capability.

This chapter, then, is about the incremental business of managing a good R&D organization.

Obviously, this approach might not always be appropriate. In the case of a very poorly performing R&D laboratory, for example, radical surgery - rather than incremental improvement - might be the best strategy. Equally obvious, even the best run R&D lab should seize the opportunity for a revolutionary gain in productivity whenever one presents itself.

ASSESSMENT - ESTABLISHING THE BASE

The point from which one starts this improvement effort is
critical, not always so much in an absolute sense as in a relative sense. Our efforts to improve must have a point of reference from which we can measure our improvement - even if
only qualitatively. Let's consider some of those "measurements," understanding that few are actually real measurements of productivity, but rather functions or attributes often
associated with it.

* Return on Investment is a popular measurement. If the
  R&D investment in a product is returned many times
  over, then the R&D was "productive." This kind of
  measurement is most applicable to Development; generally
  does not assess indirectly related returns, and measures
  history or forecasts - with risk - the future.

* Product Leadership, expressed in attributes of function,
  quality, extendability, and public indentification, is an
  important measurement of R&D productivity. It may not
  tell one the financial story; but it indicates much about
  past innovation, attention to detail, management, service,
  and public recognition.

* Competitive Position is clearly a measurement of relative
  development productivity, although it may be associated
  with many other factors as well.

* Vitality of the R&D Staff can be assessed and is always
  an important part of understanding future contribution.
  Vitality involves many factors including drive, motivation,
  education, learning, interest, and self-improvement. We
  measure it by patents, papers, products, participation,
  and development of people and ideas.

* Quality of Leadership tells us much about an organization's base, as well as its possibilities. Are the leaders
  innovative? Do they strive for excellence? Do they
  develop outstanding people? Are they sought after for
  difficult jobs? Are they recognized inside, outside, and
  within their organizations for their leadership? Questions
  such as these help in assessing the leadership base.

There are many other items which could be listed in assessing the R&D base. These include areas which make possible fruition of good R&D work. The best product in the best
laboratory will not succeed without a supporting structure of
finance, manufacturing, and marketing. In many cases, intel-

lectual leadership for a successful product is as necessary
from functions outside R&D as from within R&D. At best, we
can attempt to suggest here some items which represent things
to look for in assessing the base.

IMPROVEMENT

Based upon the above, which we will call the base management
assessment, it is now necessary to consider how the improvement program can be started. There are a number of important issues which are part of this program. Critical to it is
the belief that an R&D organization consists of highly talented
people who will be most successful and make their greatest
contributions when they are working in directions they themselves see as desirable. As a consequence, an improvement
program will be most successful if the R&D organization (lab)
itself is directly involved in designing its own improvement
program. The lab should provide its own assessment of its
base, its own view of the challenges and opportunities it
faces, and its own strengths and weaknesses and action plans.
    In this view, the first effort of management above the
R&D organization (lab) is to assure itself that the lab is good
enough as a base from which to build. The second effort of
management is then to enlist the lab in a thorough self-
assessment of its base, challenges and opportunities, strengths
and weaknesses, and action plans. It is critical that the lab
do the self-assessment; it is equally critical the management
above the lab have its own assessment. The comparison of
those assessments provides an opportunity for additional improvement. Let's consider some aspects of those comparisons:

1. Suppose the assessment of the base is dramatically dif-
    ferent in some areas. This may well indicate need for
    dialogue. In some cases, it may indicate fundamental pro-
    blems in those areas.

2. Suppose the assessment of the challenges and opportunities
    shows a poor or an unrealistic opportunity outlook.
    Again, greater understanding is required between manage-
    ment and lab.

3. Suppose that the assessment of the base, challenges and
    opportunities, and strengths and weaknesses, is performed
    well and that the action plans to improve are thoughtful
    and realistic. In that case, the management task is to
    encourage those action plans that are within the control of
    the lab, including personal support for those changes that
    are difficult because of organizational rigidity. Action

plans beyond the control of the lab must be taken seriously. Where direct management action can support lab action
plans immediately, there are substantial motivational benefits to be gained.

One can hypothesize a wide variety of other potential
scenarios. Most important to the process is that management
review the lab assessment thoughtfully and helpfully, and with
the determination to see the lab improve. The first assessment
will tell much about the lab management, as well as about the
lab. It will be a good start, at best, in a process which must
be ongoing. Having gotten the assessment - having gotten the
action plans - management must measure the results of the
plans while developing its own assessment and action plan for
the lab in the next round of assessment-analysis-action.

RELATION TO PRODUCTIVITY

Most of the items in the lab assessment are difficult to relate
to R&D productivity. This should not discourage one, since
so much of R&D must be based on judgment. Potential "improvements" must be assessed in terms of their impact on the
laboratory. Curing unimportant weaknesses may be useful,
while curing fundamental weaknesses is critical.
Potential weaknesses include skill of staff; currency of
tools; adequacy of support groups; leadership development
processes; contact with universities; motivation of staff; adequacy of market and product requirements; and vision of the
future. The list can be very long if written without knowledge of the particular lab. With that knowledge, the five or
ten most significant weaknesses can usually be identified and
jointly agreed upon. In most thoughtful studies, the major
weaknesses are less often calls for more resources than they
are an identification of the need for critical direction of
existing efforts.
Potential strength include skill of staff; maturity of staff;
product lines; company strength; leadership; leadership development; the technology base; unique tools; recruiting
capability; and present productivity. Again the list can be
very long unless one considers the particular lab in detail.
Again, it is important to determine the top ten or so of the
most important strengths so that improvement can be built from
strength.
Challenges and opportunities include extendability of the
science; application of the science; extendability of products;
extension of tools; extension of processes; training of support
groups; and applicability of tools to improve R&D productivity.
The list can be long yet again. And, again, focusing in on

the particular lab in question will inevitably produce a list of the top ten.

It is this process of analyzing the base and analyzing the opportunity, as an ongoing and measured process between management and lab, that I recommend as a tool for improving R&D productivity.

10
Mathematical Models of Science Productivity
Arthur C. Damask

The first part of this chapter reviews some empirical "laws" governing the progress of science - its growth and its quality - that have been postulated during the past two centuries.

If science itself does obey such "natural laws," it is perhaps not unreasonable to examine science from the standpoint of other general laws or theories developed by scientists, but not previously thought to apply to the discipline itself. Specifically, the second part of this chapter proposes that scientific research be cast in the framework of information theory.

SUMMARY OF SOME EXISTING MODELS

The growth of science has been a subject of investigation for at least 150 years. The usual indicators, number of scientists and number of their publications, have been shown to display empirical regularities similar to those of various other "organic ensembles" - and, conjecture has it, for much the same reasons. For example, the growth of yeast cells in a container begins rapidly but, because of food limitations, eventually saturates. The growth of science is also rapid; but, because of the limitations of manpower and capital, it too must saturate. The first part of this chapter reviews some of these basic models, or "laws" of behavior, of science.

Adams' Law of Exponential Growth

Exponential growth was well known in the eighteenth century, but Henry Adams (1838-1918) was apparently the first to ob-

serve that it applied to science. Actually, he stated that the
annual percentage increase in levels of scientific effort remains
constant in time. For example, figure 10.1 shows the membership in the American Association for the Advancement of
Science (AAAS) from 1875 to 1975. A similar count from A-
merican Men of Science shows an exponential growth rate compounding at 6 percent per year. A rule of thumb by bankers
is that 72 divided by a compounding interest rate yields the
doubling time. Thus 72/6% = 12 years. This is not the worldwide rate, though; in the United Kingdom the rate up to 1970
was 4.5 percent per year. This increasing number of scientists has produced an increased amount of scientific literature.
Figure 10.2 shows the number of "Physics Abstracts" from
1900 to 1950. Except for interruptions during the two world
wars, these have also been increasing exponentially with a
doubling time also of about 12 years. The recognized sub-
fields of science, which are themselves fragmenting into sub-
groups, can also be examined individually. As Figure 10.3
shows, all have a doubling time of 15 years. This fragmenta-
tion of fields created a need for new scientific journals.
Figure 10.4 shows the increase in numbers of journals from
1665 to 1950 and, in the inset, the number of abstract journals
from 1830 to 1950. Both are increasing at a rate of 5 percent
per year, implying a doubling time of about 14 to 15 years.
As equipment to feed the new discoveries becomes more complex, it is also more costly. Figure 10.5 shows the increase in
cost of frontier nuclear magnetic resonance (NMR) equipment
from 1950 to 1970. This particular example shows a doubling
rate of about 4.75 years or a 15 percent annual growth rate.
Almost any statistical data of science taken over a sufficient
period of time have shown an essentially exponential growth
rate.

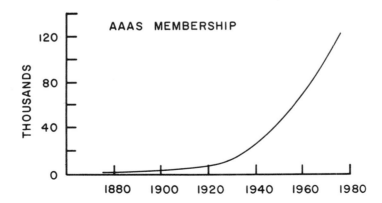

Fig. 10.1. AAAS membership for the past century as an ex-
          ample of exponential growth.

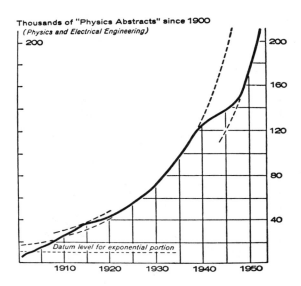

Fig. 10.2.   Thousands of Physics Abstract 1900-1960.   This
             illustrates exponential growth displaced by war
             years.

SOURCE: Price, Science Since Babylon (New Haven: Yale
          University Press, 1975).

Verhulst's Law of Growth Saturation

It is clear that nothing can continue an exponential growth
rate forever.   In 1838, P.F. Verhulst modified the exponential
growth law.   He suggested, in a population study, that although the rate of growth of a population p was indeed proportional to the population present at any time, it was also
proportional to the food supply a.   The food supply diminished
as the population increased.   Thus, the available food supply
at any time was (a-p).   Therefore, the time rate of change of
the population would be

$$\frac{dp}{dt} = bp \ (a-p),$$

which integrates to

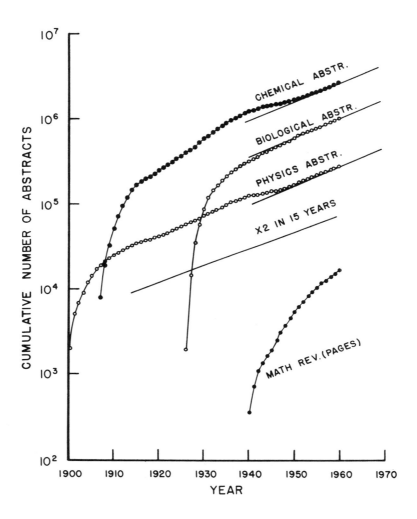

Fig. 10.3. Semilog plot of number of abstracts in separate fields.

SOURCE: Price, Science Since Babylon.

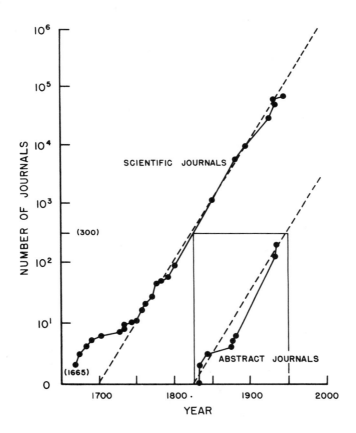

Fig. 10.4.   Semilog plot of number of scientific journals from
              1665-1950 and number of abstract journals in inset.

SOURCE: Price, Science Since Babylon.

$$p = \frac{a}{1 + e^{-ab(t+k)}} \ ,$$

where b is a constant representing the growth rate and k is a
constant of integration that determines the origin of the curve.
This is the familiar S-curve called a "logistic" curve. Almost

all growth paths take this shape, although sometimes with a skew. Yeast cells; plant stalks (see figure 10.6); humans from birth to adulthood; and even the inanimate growth of a crystal must follow a logistic curve if the nutrient supply is limited.

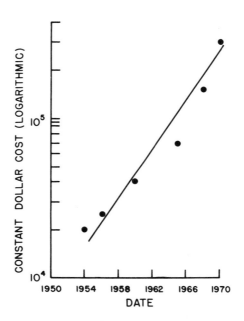

Fig. 10.5.   Semilog plot of cost increase of NMR equipment at the technological frontier.

SOURCE: Bromley et al., Physics in Perspective: Student Edition (Washington, D.C.: National Research Council-National Academy of Sciences, 1973).

The curve also finds application in a variety of statistical studies. For example, the rate of diffusion of hybrid corn from its discovery to its use in several U.S. states is shown in figure 10.7. (The nutrient for growth in this case is the remaining available land). Sometimes data must be considered in two or more separate parts. An example is shown in figure 10.8 for growth in the number of universities. The medieval religious form began in Cairo in 950 and an exponential growth occurred, doubling about every 100 years. Around 1460, the

Renaissance type of university was begun and entered exponential growth, doubling about every 65 years, while the
number of older religious universities reached saturation.

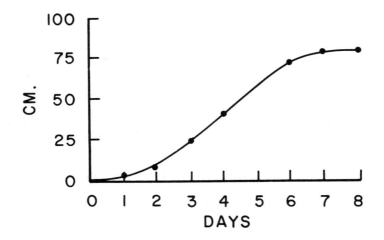

Fig. 10.6.   Growth in length of a beanstalk as a function of
             age.

SOURCE: Thompson, D'Arcy, Growth and Form (Cambridge:
        Cambridge University Press, 1948).

St. Simon's Law of Pulsed Growth

Claude Henri de St. Simon (1760-1825) was a French social
philosopher. In his view, the development of people or nations is characterized by periods of innovation and construction followed by periods of consolidation and evaluation.
These periods were called "synthetic" and "analytic," respec-
tively. (The "Kondratieff" or "Forrester" cycles discussed by
D. Bruce Merrifield would also seem to be an example of this
general model. See Chapter 7.) A plot of any human activity
on the basis of this model would be a growth curve which, as
it approaches saturation, would initiate another growth curve
as new concepts or innovations are introduced. A schematic
of such behavior is shown in figure 10.9. An example of this
in technology is the increase in energy of new designs of
accelerators shown in figure 10.10: each new innovation has
its life cycle. Another manifestation of this is the pervasive
interest in the "newness" of science. M.M. Kessler (quoted

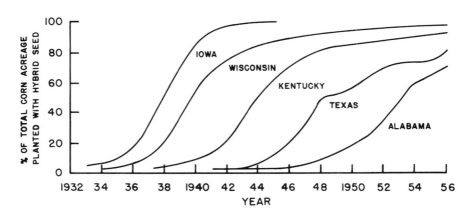

Fig. 10.7.   Rate of diffusion of hybrid corn in various States.

SOURCE: Griliches, Z.   Econometrica, 1957, p. 502.

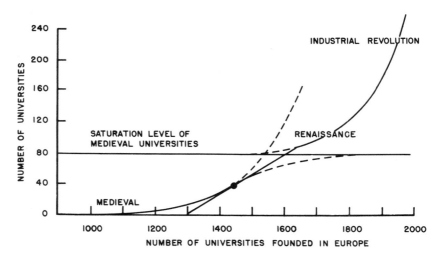

Fig. 10.8.   Growth of number of universities.   The medieval,
or religious oriented, exhibits a logistic curve,
while   the   Renaissance   type   is   still   increasing
exponentially.

SOURCE: Price, Science Since Babylon.

by Holton) found that 50 percent of the references cited in
<u>Physical Review</u> papers (over the period studied) are less than
three years old, and only 20 percent are more than seven
years old.

Holton used this development pattern of innovative concepts to illustrate another pattern of behavior (see figure
10.11). Here the amount of remaining interesting ideas in a

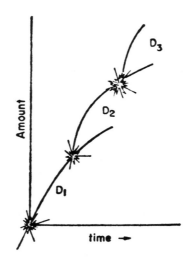

Fig. 10.9.   Schematic of amount of effort as a function of time
             expended in new ideas.

<u>SOURCE</u>: Holton, <u>Excellence and Leadership in a Democracy</u>.

new field is essentially the mirror image of the applied ideas,
with a suitable time lag. When knowledge of an innovative
concept diffuses, more scientists begin to work in the field
and the number of participants increases. As the number of
new ideas within the innovation becomes exhausted, increasing
numbers of scientists leave the field for other innovative
areas. In view of the seven-year active period of a new field
from Kessler's study, a scientist may expect to work in a
number of fields during his professional life span. The important question, however, is when to move to another field or,
in accordance with a research director's responsibility, when
to shift personnel. Journal publication has a lag time, and
most innovative ideas are spread through personal communication, conferences, or preprints. There is a further lag, for
an interested researcher has to learn details, set up new ex-

periments, and phase out his current work. Thus, by the
time the peak of participation in figure 10.11 is reached, the
field is already in the declining phase. If a laboratory does
not have some of its researchers in the frontier of research
either as innovators or rapid recipients of innovative ideas, it
will always be behind and its usefulness will be limited.

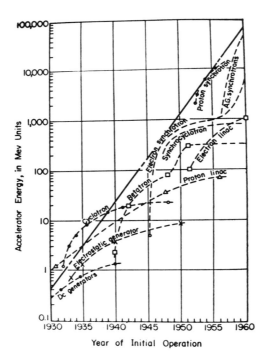

Year of Initial Operation

Fig. 10.10.   SOURCE: M.S. Livingston and J. Blewett, Parti-
cle Accelerators (New York: McGraw-Hill 1962).

Lehman's Measure of the Age-Productivity Relation

It is by now well know that a scientist has his most productive
years while he is young.   H.G. Lehman (1954) collected data
of the yearly publication records of about 60 eminent scientists
and mathematicians from many different countries.   These all
fall on a universal curve with very little deviation.   An example curve is shown in figure 10.12, which shows the data
for the United States as compared with 14 small countries.
Similar data from other large countries also closely follow these

curves. One might argue that the reason for the decline after age 40 is that productive time consumed by teaching, directing, committee work, etc. - not that older scientists suffer a death of brain cells or invariably become conservative. The

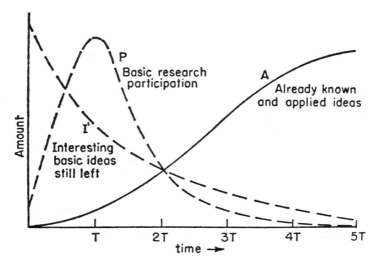

Fig. 10.11.   Relationship of time-rate of entry of participants into a new field of basic research.

SOURCE: Holton, Excellence and Leadership in a Democracy.

decline in productivity does not mean a decline in scientific usefulness, for activities like teaching and committee participation are necessary for the health of science.

Shockley's Log-Normal Data of Scientific Productivity

William Shockley, in 1957, examined the publications of scientific personnel at five laboratories (Brookhaven National Laboratory; Atomic and Radiation Physics Division of the National Bureau of Standards (NBS); Los Alamos Scientific Laboratory; the Physics Department of Columbia University; and a large industrial laboratory). He counted the number of papers per man over a four-year period and reduced each by the appropriate fraction whenever an individual had co-authors. He found that some individuals create science (i.e., write papers) at a rate of 50 times greater than others, and that the normal distribution function did not apply. Instead, he showed, it is the logarithm of the scientific production index that obeys a normal distribution function. For example, the logarithm of publications and patents vs. personnel at a division of the National Bureau of Standards over a period of 5.7 years is shown in figure 10.13. Plotting the logarithm of publications on probability graph paper results in a straight line, which substantiates the log-normal distribution function.

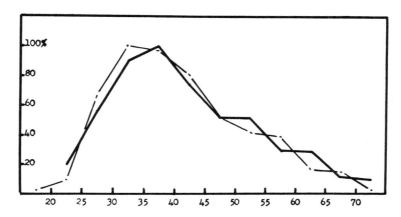

Fig. 10.12. Creative production rate in science and mathematics vs. age for U.S. (dashed line) and for nationals of 14 small countries (solid line).

SOURCE: Lehman, Sci. Monthly 78 (1954): 321.

In an attempt to explain this normal distribution of the logarithm of scientific productivity, Shockley made three (not unrelated) conjectures about the nature of mental activity.

1. He considered Rashevsky's idea that there is some attribute of the human brain that allows an individual to be aware of m ideas and their relationships. Then the number of combinations of these ideas that he can think about is m-factorial. Thus, if a concept required a combination of two separate thoughts, the man with m = 2 can conceive of them in two separate ways, i.e., (1,2) or (2,1) while a man with m=3 can conceive of them along with a third, irrelevant, idea in six separate ways, giving a three-fold advantage. In a complex problem, a man with m = 11 has an 11-fold advantage over one with m = 10. Thus, a 10 percent increase in mental ability gives rise to an 1,100 percent increase in mental output.

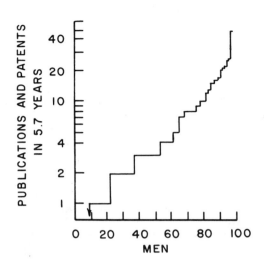

Fig. 10.13.   Semilog plot of cumulative distribution of pub-
             lications and patents at NBS.

SOURCE: Shockley.

    2.   Scientific productivity may be a product of several
independent factors, e.g., ability to think up a problem;
ability to work on it; ability to interpret the data; ability to
write a paper; etc.   If these probability factors, called F_1,
F_2, etc., are independent, then the total probability P is the
joint probability of the factors or $P = F_1 F_2 F_3 F_4 \ldots F_N$.   Suppose there are four factors.   If another individual has a 50
percent greater ability, then his advantage is a factor of five
greater, viz.,

$$\frac{P\ (1.5)}{P\ (1)} = \frac{(1.5\ F_1)\ (1.5\ F_2)\ (1.5\ F_3)\ (1.5\ F_4)}{F_1\ F_2\ F_3\ F_4} = 5$$

This formulation may well result in the observed log-normal
distribution because

$$\log P = \log F_1 + \log F_2 + \log F_3 + \log F_4;$$

and if each of the Fs varies independently, then their sum will
have a normal distribution and so will the logarithm of their
productivity.

3. Suppose each brain i has a "mental temperature" T_i and a given problem s has a "potential barrier" U_s one must surmount in order to solve it. Then, by analogy with chemical rate equations, an individual's rate of production is

$$p\ (i,s) = p_s \exp\ (-U_s/k\ T_i),$$

where p_s is the rate constant. If T_i obeys a normal distribution, then p(i) will obey a log-normal one. Shockley reported that he had insufficient data to evaluate this interpretation, and apparently nothing has been done on it since 1957.

Rousseau's Law of Quality

When one examines the quality Q of a given quantity q, he often finds that quality varies as the square root of quantity: $Q = q^{\frac{1}{2}}$. This relationship is often referred to as Rousseau's Law, after Jean-Jacques Rousseau (1712-1778). Although Rousseau states the proposition clearly, no data for the conclusion can be found in his writings. Francis Galton (1822-1911) was apparently the first to gather extensive data to confirm this relationship. For example, Galton examined the select notices in the obituaries in the London Times and calculated that there were about 3,000 eminent persons out of the English population of some nine million. N. Rescher points out that, of 1,600 educational institutions in the United States which grant the baccalaureate degree, only about 40 are really "major" universities.

Why such a relationship should apply is not clear, but two results from physical statistics may be useful in a philosophical consideration of Rousseau's Law. One is that, as is well known, the statistical accuracy of data improves as the square root of the amount of data. The second is that, in signal communication, the quality of the message, called signal-to-noise ratio, is equal to the square root of the number of events in the signal. We will see in the next section, however, that Rousseau's Law is only a division of a more general law.

Zipf's Law of Evaluative Distribution

Although Rousseau's Law may be useful as a rule of thumb, it is clear that there is a degree of arbitrariness involved in selecting the number of important persons or events. George Zipf (1949) has shown that the relative evaluation of objects is operative to a wide variety of human distributions and behavior.

Suppose we define a quality level of findings as λ where $0 \leq \lambda \leq 1$. The number of items (or events) of quality λ, called $Q(\lambda)$, will be proportional to quantity to the power of λ, or $q\lambda$. Thus,

$$Q\ (\lambda) = q\lambda,$$

and Rousseau's Law is the special case of $\lambda = \frac{1}{2}$. If $\lambda = 1$ then $Q\ (\lambda) = q$, and all the events are uniformly undistinguished. If λ is $\frac{1}{4}$, then we seek the refined quality level of Rousseau's quality. That is, by Rousseau's law,

$$Q\ (\tfrac{1}{4}) = [Q(\tfrac{1}{2})]^{\frac{1}{2}} = q^{\frac{1}{4}}.$$

Taking the log of both sides, we have

$$\log\ Q\ (\tfrac{1}{4}) = \tfrac{1}{4}\ \log\ q.$$

This suggests that, in general, λ is the ratio of the logarithm of the number of "quality" events to the logarithm of the total number of events, viz.,

$$\frac{\log\ Q\ (\lambda)}{\log\ q} = \lambda\ \cdot$$

It might be helpful to think in terms of a number of discrete "merit groups." If we continue as above and choose four such groups, then the first quality group is $\lambda = \frac{1}{2}$, the second is $\lambda = \frac{1}{4}$, the third is $\lambda = 1/8$, and the highest is $\lambda = 1/16$. The numbers in each merit group for q events would be

- lowest: $\log\ Q\ (1/2) = 1/2\ \log\ q$

- second: $\log\ Q\ (1/4) = 1/4\ \log\ q$

- third: $\log\ Q\ (1/8) = 1/8\ \log\ q$

- highest: $\log\ Q\ (1/16) = 1/16\ \log\ q$

If λ is small, the degree of quality is high, and a plot of $\log\ Q\ (\lambda)/\log\ q = \lambda$ is linear. Such a plot with arbitrary coordinates is shown in figure 10.14. Using such a plot, one can directly estimate the amount of quality data for any degree of quality.

We have viewed the quantity of science q as if it were a lake or reservoir of knowledge from which some samples contain a higher quality of information than others. A better analogy would be a reservoir that is being constantly enlarged through an influx of new water. The evidence of a widespread tendency not to refer to older publications suggests that there is also leakage from the reservoir.

The rate of increase of the quantity of knowledge has been shown to be exponential. Suppose this rate is b. Then at any time after t_0,

$q = q_0 e^{bt}$, where q_0 is the initial quantity.

The quality amount becomes

$Q(\lambda) = q_0\lambda\ e^{\lambda bt}$,

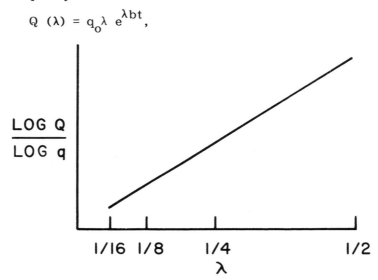

Fig. 10.14.   Semilog plot of fraction of high quality findings Q over routine findings q vs. λ, where a large λ means low quality.

where the first factor on the right is Zipf's Law for still water.

As shown earlier, the quantity of scientific knowledge, i.e., number of publications, is growing at the rate of 5 percent per year. This implies that $Q(\frac{1}{2})$ is increasing at the rate of 2.5 percent per year, $Q(\frac{1}{4})$ at 1.25 percent, and so forth.

What can be said about really "first-rate" discoveries F, those which change the course of science and technology, as indicated in figure 10.9? Rescher (1978) has discussed data which indicate that, over many years, the quantity F remained constant at a very small number and, as science grew, F increased very slowly. He therefore suggested the empirical relation

$F \propto \log q$.

From above, the growth of science was $q = q_0 \exp(bt)$, so

$$F \propto \log q_0 + bt,$$

and the rate of growth of F with time is a constant dependent upon the rate of growth of scientific knowledge. This relation, although not part of Zipf's Law, is consistent with the observations of the rate of accumulation of first-rate discoveries.

The growth of science is dependent on both labor and capital. Therefore, the growth rate exponential is actually

$$b = b_\ell + b_c.$$

Because these are exponents, the larger one will dominate. Although the cost of equipment is increasing exponentially, the volume of its cost cannot yet be significant because the growth rate of science of five percent is close to the growth rate of scientific manpower of six percent, as shown above.

INFORMATION THEORY   AS A MEASURE OF RESEARCH PRODUCTIVITY

The need for measures of productivity is increasing as planners, economists and elected officials attempt to allocate resources. In some cases the measurement of productivity is straightforward, such as bushels of grain per acre or tons of steel per dollar of capitalization and/or operating costs. Such measurement becomes more difficult when intangibles are involved. The research productivity of a laboratory, particularly in its value to a company or government department, can usually be measured only in retrospect, but experienced research managers are generally able to evaluate and direct a laboratory by methods that are either intuitive or at least not often articulated. Nevertheless, a more precise technique for measuring and predicting research productivity would be of considerable value to a research director in the selection of an optimal course of action or in making changes in organizational structure, manpower, or projects. It is in this context that a fresh examination of Information Theory may be in order.

Information Theory was developed in the 1940s by Shannon (Shannon and Weaver, 1949), following the pioneering work of Norbert Wiener. Originally formulated for -- and still used largely in -- the study of message transmission through telecommunications systems, Information Theory is closely related mathematically to the notion of entropy in thermodynamics; indeed, one often hears the phrase "entropy of information." The reason for this close connection is that both fields are concerned with randomness -- thermodynamics with the randomness of the arrangement of atoms or molecules and Information Theory with the randomness of symbols in a message.

The elegance of the mathematical formulation quickly led to a proliferation of attempts to extend Information Theory beyond the field of communications. One area of early interest was the management of research laboratories. But, as is often the case, early exuberance resulted in extravagant claims - that the research director, for example, could now safely be eliminated in a favor of a computer. The swift rejection of such claims put a damper on further attempts to extend the formalism in this direction.

During the past fifteen years, however, there has been a resurgent interest in examining the potential breadth of Information Theory. For example, Moles (1966) summarized a wide body of work in Europe on the planning of concert programs with the aid of Information Theory. Cherry (1966) extended these thoughts further and called attention to the wide study for the past two centuries on non-event-related probability theory. It appears that, while the extravagant claims for application to research productivity were justifiably rejected, the application of Information Theory to a more limited role in the measurement of research certainly merits reexamination.

Information Theory

Shannon recognized that there exist degrees of order-disorder in communication. An English word has a higher degree of order than does an equal number of letters randomly chosen. A sentence has a higher degree of order than does the same number of words randomly chosen from a book. In this sense, the concept of entropy is applicable in communication. To see this, consider the quantity W defined in statistical mechanics as:

$$W = \frac{\text{number of states identical with the one considered}}{\text{total number of possible states}} .$$

Although originally formulated for an atomistic approach to thermodynamics, the word states used here can cover any comparable situation. For example, the occurrence of a specified letter in a group is a state.

If there are only 26 letters, each has an equal probability of being selected from a bin containing one each of the letters of the alphabet. But if the bin contains letters in proportion to the frequency of English usage, then 18 out of every 100 will probably be the letter e. Thus, W above for e will be

18/100.   It is well known to cryptographers that the relative occurrence of the most common letters of the alphabet in the English language by decreasing frequency is E T O A N I R S H D L, with Z, X and Q at the lowest frequencies.   A cryptographer trying to decipher a message in which only the most frequently occurring letters are used will have a difficult time. However, if a Z occurs his task will be easier because this is an unexpected occurrence, i.e., one with low probability (or high improbability).   Without this event the cryptographer is taught nothing; with the occurrence of this unexpected event, the cryptographer gains information useful to cracking the code.   Hence, we may say that the originality or unexpectedness of an event is a function of the improbability of its occurrence.   This is the essential point of Information Theory - more information (or higher degree of unexpectedness) is obtained from events of low probability.

By analogy with the statistical formulation of entropy (see, for example, Rushbrooke, 1949), Shannon expressed the relationship of information, H, to the degree of probability W as:

$$H = - K \log W, \tag{1}$$

where K is a constant.   Since probability is less than unity, the log will be negative; the minus sign assures that the information content of a message will be a positive quantity.

A unit of information can be made to correspond to a difference between two choices; yes or no, on or off, 0 or 1. Any more complicated questions can be reduced to a series of two-choice questions.   In a two-choice question there is only one answer, and the a priori probability is $\frac{1}{2}$ for either. Equation (1) is then

$$H = - K \log \tfrac{1}{2} = K \log 2.$$

A useful alternative form is obtained by using logarithms to the base 2, which allows K to be set equal to unity and which yields H in units of information (a "bit" in communication terminology):

$$H = - \log_2 W. \tag{2}$$

The information content of a set of probabilities is calculated in the following way.   Suppose, for example, there are only three symbols (1, 2, and 3) being produced by a source with respective probabilities $P(1)$, $P(2)$, and $P(3)$.   Since 1 occurs only $P(1)$ of the time, 2 occurs $P(2)$ of the time and 3 occurs $P(3)$ of the time, the average information of all three is, from Equation (2),

$$H = - \left[P(1) \log_2 P(1) + P(2) \log_2 P(2) + P(3) \log_2 P(3) \right],$$

where the probabilities are relative since their sum must be unity. The above sum may be written as

$$H = - \sum_{i=1}^{3} P_i \log_2 P_i$$

or, dropping the subscript 2 for simplification of writing and extending to any given number of elements n, the Shannon equation becomes

$$H = - \sum_{i=1}^{n} P_i \log P_i, \tag{3}$$

which represents the number of bits of information per symbol. If the source is producing information at rate N bits per unit time for a time t, i.e., Nt is the message length, Equation (3) is simply

$$H = - Nt \sum_{i=1}^{n} P_i \log P_i \tag{4}$$

The rate of information R is H/t; and, if the source rate is $N = 1$, i.e., one symbol per unit time, then

$$R = \sum_{i=1}^{n} P_i \log P_i \quad \text{bits per symbol per unit time.} \tag{5}$$

(Note that setting $N = 1$ is introduced only for simplification.) If all P_i's are equal, then Equation (3) is

$$H_m = - \sum_{i=1}^{n} 1/n \log 1/n$$

$$= -\log 1/n$$

$$= \log n. \tag{6}$$

It can be proven that H_m is maximum for this situation [See, for example, Raisbeck(1964)]. For any other situation the ratio H/H_m is the relative information of the message and the quantity $(1 - H/H_m)$ is the redundancy of the message. It should be noted that redundancy is not wasted because some repitition assures accuracy. All human languages have redundancy values estimated at 40 ± 10 percent.

Information Theory is formulated on the basis of probability theory, and many of the early criticisms of using Information Theory in the laboratory context revolved around the applicability of probabilistic concepts to quantities like expected research results. It is worth considering the two most basic of these criticisms, for the weight of scholarship tends to show, I believe, that research may indeed be treated with a probabilistic formulation.

1. Probability is event related, as in coin tossing, dice rolling, letter frequency in an alphabet, etc. How can the probability formalism be adapted to non-event situations such as betting on a horse race or backing scientific expectations with money or manpower?
2. If such a non-event-related probability distribution were constructed, how could the relative information content of disparate activities such as chemical research, physical research, or engineering developments possibly be established?

The first criticism has been answered by a number of scholars who have considered it, from Bayes in 1793 through Good (1950) and Carnap (1950). What was required was a redefinition of the ambiguous word "probability." A distinction was made between <u>statistical</u> probability and <u>inductive</u> probability. The former is the common usage in which we have knowledge from previous experience of the chances of outcome, e.g., 50-50 in tossing a coin. In the latter, which may be applied to research, we do not have prior experience but we can make judgments of probabilities. For example, will a new material be an electrical conductor or not? Carnap has called this the Principle of Indifference and has sharpened the theory of inductive probability into a tool of research as precise as statistical probability. As further experience is gained a subjective probability enters. For example, improved judgment not on whether a new material will be an electrical conductor or not but on how good it will be compared to other conductors will alter the expectation of outcome.

Thus, we can view a scientist as having laboratory observations that provide him with the evidence he needs to place "odds" on various explanatory hypotheses. Further evidence may tend to confirm some hypotheses and weaken faith in others - and therefore change the odds. What is implied by this is that, although a fixed distribution of "odds" on the experiments in a laboratory may have limited usefulness by itself, a continuous flow of data from experiments will alter that distribution and the associated information content. It is therefore possible to use the intuitive judgment of a laboratory director, which Carnap has argued to be quantifiable, as a basis for a probability distribution - and hence for information content via the Shannon equation.

Criticism (2) is easier to address once we reject the idea that information theory can yield absolute information. It can yield only relative information, because the probabilities in the equations are relative. Therefore, under this view, there is very little basis for trying to compare the probabilities of success, or "forseeability," of an engineering development project with the understanding, gained through research, of a scientific hypothesis. It is clearly a situation of trying to compare apples and oranges. The concept of a laboratory as an information transmitter and the company as a receiver must first be modified to the actual situation. The various parts of a laboratory transmit to various parts of a company or organization. If these subsets of laboratory transmission are considered, then relative "probabilities" or "expectations" or "degrees of forseeability" are most readily compared and information content evaluated. The absolute information values of these subsets cannot be compared by means of any present theory and, therefore, the information content of a chemical laboratory cannot be compared with (say) that of a semiconductor laboratory.

What is of interest – and what seems not to have been studied either experimentally or theoretically – is the addition properties of entropy. Since the total information content is the sum of the entropies of the various distributions, and the information is a function of the logarithm of a distribution, then the results of the additions of various organizational structures of a given laboratory will vary. The sums will vary more with organizational structure than with possible errors in probability assignments, since it is logarithms of the latter that enter into the calculation and a logarithm is a slowly varying function.

Application to Research

Let us assume that there is one person working on each project, so that n represents either person or a project. We will calculate the information content per unit informational output Nt for labs of sizes 4, 8, 16, 24, 32 and 48 with some different relative probabilities among the projects. We will first calculate the informational content H/Nt if the probability of outcome is the same for each project. We will then hold half of the projects constant at the same probability and let the other half have higher expectations of outcome, namely, 5, 10, 20 and 50 times more probable than the other half. Equation (3) is used with the sum of probabilities being set equal to unity.

A plot of the six labs of different sizes is shown in figure 10.15, where the numbers on the right indicate the relative probability of the work in half of the laboratories compared to the other half. It should be noted that: (1) the sum of two labs with four projects does not equal that of a lab with eight projects, etc., and (2) this "organizational" sensitivity is much greater than the sensitivity to the relative probability estimates. The dashed line is an arbitrarily chosen constant H.

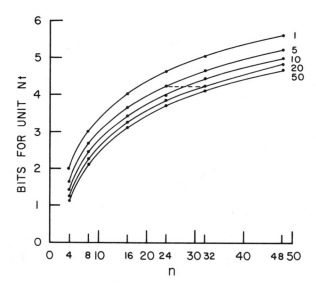

Fig. 10.15.   Bits of information per unit Nt produced by n projects with half having greater predictability than the other half by the amounts indicated on the right side of the curves. The dashed line shows an example of a constant level of information for two lab sizes with different predictability factors.

It shows that, if some members are shifted to work on projects with a higher expectation of outcome, the lab size must increase accordingly to maintain the same value of H.

Also of interest in the internal evaluation of a laboratory is the information per unit output per man (project). To obtain this quantity, the information is divided by n for each point. This is seen in figure 10.16, which shows how the bits-per-project change with both lab size and the relative probability of the outcomes of the projects. A low saturation is seen for large labs.

Applying this model to a laboratory over a several-year period might conceivably require that data be collected con-

tinuously. Every time there is a change in organization, manpower, project, or expectation, a recalculation must be made.
These calculations are not difficult and could be readily pro-
grammed for a computer. In some cases interdependence exists and a modified calculation must be made.

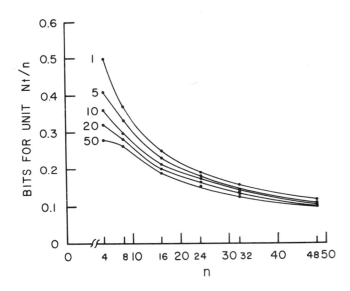

Fig. 10.16. Bits for unit Nt per project for the five cate-
           gories of fig. 10.1.

Quality, Quantity, and Rate of Research

A company is a receptor of the research transmitted by the
laboratory. Equation (3) can be used to give some quantitative measures of the three important parameters of research:
quality, quantity, and rate.
    In the previous section, the P_i were used interchangeably
as both projects and persons with the assumption that one
person worked on only one project. These concepts should
normally be separated, however. One person may work on
several different projects and the rate of research production
N is a function of the number of persons. (This rate of production depends also on the quality of the personnel.)
    A given company has a certain rate at which it can ab-
sorb new research, that is, a rate at which it can modify its

operations.   If we call the rate of research absorption of a
company H/t = R and the rate of research production R$'$, then
an important consideration of a company can be called the
value of the research to the company.   Although value may
simplistically be considered as monetary return, it should be
noted that there exist less tangible values, e.g., patent position, etc.   Nevertheless, we may write

$$\text{value} = f(R - R').\qquad\qquad(7)$$

Considering for now that value is monetary return, Equation
(7) represents the manufacturing change rate or growth rate
in new products a company must have in order to utilize the
research output.   If a change in this value only is desired,
then either the number of research personnel or the originality
level may be varied.   With a suitable choice of parameters,
this formulation may lead to quantitative evaluation of procedures of laboratory management that have long been known
only intuitively.   A useful first approximation of the function
in Equation (7) is probably the reciprocal of the absolute
difference, $1 / |R' - R|$, making value behave as does a reso-
nance function.
     One item that has been neglected so far is the qualitative
level of the receptor (company).   A research company in the
seventeenth century may discover Newton's laws of motion as
an unexpected event with a corresponding large H, while an
American space company would not assign a large H to anything less than a faster algorithm for solving Newton's laws for
spaceships.   For this reason, the R of Equation (7) must be
considered to follow a learning curve and, to maintain a constant value, R must follow the same curve.   That is, for a
constant perception of usefulness, the research level must
increase at the same rate as the sophistication of the company's processes and personnel.

Productivity of Research

The model, which is concerned with quantity and quality of
research output, may also be useful in considerations of financial health of companies, industrial sectors, or of the national
economy.   These effects involve the impact of research results; but, in order to have an impact, a research result must
be utilized.   An often-quoted number is that research is only
10 percent of the costs of a new product or manufacturing
method.   The remaining 90 percent is largely for development
and marketing.   Therefore, a research result must compete for
available capital and corporate interest, both of which change
with time.   For these reasons, a time-varying fraction of research results enters the economy.

In view of this, the effect of research on corporate or national productivity must include in the analysis the amount of research results developed, in addition to the quantity and quality of research. Such analysis appears to be feasible.

CONCLUSION

It seems worthwhile to track a laboratory over time, as accumulated research results change probabilities and reorganizations change structure. One can establish a method to compare expectation with output over time. One could also analyze the historic structure and results of a laboratory over, say, the past decade, although the accuracy of such a backward-looking procedure would depend on recollections by individuals of their expectations at various times during the course of the research.

What can be gained by this effort is the following. Most all of the above-cited studies are attempts to explain the cerebration processes of the human mind in making judgments. Having established a symbolic or mathematical representation of this, one can work out a quantification or relative numerical assignment. Thus, although such quantification would not change the judgment processes of research directors, it would give them an additional tool. With a series of options available as a function of time for organizational changes, personnel reassignments, new programs, etc., it becomes possible to make quantitative estimates of the relative changes in the information output of the research for each of these options.

REFERENCES

1. Bromley, D. A. et al. 1973. Physics in Perspective: Student Edition, Washington, D.C.: National Research Council - National Academy of Sciences.

2. Cherry, C. 1966. On Human Communication, Cambridge, Mass: MIT Press.

3. Good, I. J. 1950. Probability and the Weighing of Evidence. London: Charles Griffin Ltd.

4. Griliches, Z. 1957. "Hybrid Corn: An Exploration in the Economics of Technical Change." Econometrica, 25, p. 502.

5. Holton, G. 1962. "Models for Understanding the Growth and Excellence of Science." In S. R. Graubard and G. Holton, eds., Excellence and Leadership in a Democracy, New York: Columbia University Press.

6. Lehman, H. G. 1954. "Men's Creative Production Rates at Different Ages and in Different Countries." Scientific Monthy 78:321.

7. Moles, A. 1966. Information Theory and Esthetic Perception. Urbana: University of Illinois Press.

8. Norris, K, and Vaizey, J. 1973. The Economics of Research and Technology. London: Allen and Unwin.

9. Price, D. de S. 1963. Little Science, Big Science. New York: Columbia University Press.

_____. 1975. Science Since Babylon. New Haven: Yale University Press.

11. Raisbeck, G. 1964. Information Theory. Cambridge: MIT Press.

12. Rashevsky, N. 1962. Mathematical Biophysics. New York: Dover.

13. Rescher, N. 1978. Scientific Progress. Pittsburgh: University of Pittsburgh Press.

14. Rushbrooke, G. S. 1949. Introduction to Statistical Mechanics. London: Oxford University Press.

15. Shannon, C. E., and Weaver, W. 1949. The Mathematical Theory of Communication. Urbana: University of Illinois Press.

16. Shockley, W. 1957. "On the Statistics of Individual Variations of Productivity in Research Laboratories." Institute of Radio Engineers, 45:281.

17. Thompson, D'A. 1948. Growth and Form. Cambridge: Cambridge University Press.

18. Zipf, G. K. 1949. Human Behavior and the Principle of Least Effort. Cambridge, Mass: Addison-Wesley.

11

Productivity of Research and Development: Summary and Perspectives

Alfred H. Nissan

This book on productivity of research and development in the industrial sector of our society has covered fields wider than those bounded by its title. Besides the specific theme of R&D productivity, our discussions ranged over the productivity of science and technology in general; planning strategies in a highly inflationary economic environment; studies on innovation; and several other aspects of the technological enterprise by which science and technology affects our social, economic and cultural welfare. I believe each contribution is worthy of deeper study and evaluation than could be given to it in these chapters.

With such broad fields cultivated by such eminent experts, it was no surprise to find a bumper crop of important facts and challenging ideas. There were no major controversies to be resolved nor opposites to be reconciled. On the other hand, there were no repetitive hammerings on any one strategy, philosophy, or theme. But there was unanimity on one single issue.

BEYOND OUR GRASP

It was unanimously agreed that the definition, evaluation, regulation or control of the productivity of industrial R&D are all well beyond our grasp. The productivity of academic, institutional, and governmental R&D is equally elusive of definition, evaluation, regulation, or control. It follows that to speak of the productivity of national R&D in science and technology is an exercise in composing fanciful fiction.

This unanimity of opinion emerged in two forms. It was explicitly stated by those authors who addressed the theme of

R&D productivity. It was implicitly espoused by those authors who addressed subjects other than R&D productivity and who studiously avoided being drawn into this thorny briar patch.

Those who directed their studies to the theme of R&D productivity stressed various types of difficulties on the way. They highlighted the fact that most assessments of R&D productivity are necessarily qualitative in view of the paucity of quantitative measures available. As Roberta Miller stressed in her very careful analysis of the problems encountered in trying to assess the productivity of R&D, there is not even a common metric by which to measure it. I shall not try here to repeat the findings by Herb Fusfeld, Dick Nelson, Roberta Miller, Arthur Anderson, and the other authors who made a brave attempt to grasp the nettle of this subject. Nor will I summarize the intriguing thoughts and suggestions made by Art Damask, who uses information theory as a tool to get hold of the idea of the productivity of R&D. These chapters are all available for you to study and evaluate, and you do not need me as an intermediary to explain or criticize them.

SOME PERSONAL CONCLUSIONS

Instead, perhaps you will allow me to integrate what I have learnt from these chapters into three strictly personal conclusions. This may encourage you to formulate your own set of conclusions explicitly, and to let the rest of us have the benefit of your thoughts on this important but elusive subject.

My first conclusion is that "productivity" is an inappropriate word to apply to the research and development activity. I have three reasons for this.

First, the word "productivity" is a well-known, much-used technical term with the precise quantitative connotation of a ratio of output measures of an activity to the measures of input directly correlated with or known to have causal relationships to the output. "Productivity," as a term, belongs to the class that includes such phrases as "Carnot Cycle Efficiency," "Quantum efficiency of a photovoltaic cell," or "the 50 percent lethal dose of a toxin." The use of such phrases implies a strict adherence to their precise technical meaning. Otherwise, their value as meaningful words degenerates, and the language is poorer by such debasement. In language, as in coinage, the bad will drive out the good.

In using these and similar terms, one is asserting that a quantitative measure is being used to assess the ratio of numerable measurable output quantity to a similarly countable or measurable input quantity that has a known or demonstrable relationship to the output. If we cannot measure the output or the input, or both, and if we cannot be certain of, or we cannot demonstrate a correlational or causal relationship between, what we consider output and input, then to use such words is a disservice to knowledge and a debasement of the coinage of language. Now, for R&D activities, the authors were unanimous in agreeing that we do not as yet know what and how to measure as "outputs" or "inputs," or how to measure them. Nor are we sure of the essential relationships between what we perceive as inputs and outputs. I believe, therefore, that we should not use a precisely defined technical word as "productivity" for what we are seeking. We should try other terms. I shall return to this matter later.

A second reason to avoid the use of the word "productivity" is the following. In our culture, "productivity" is a highly valued attribute or parameter of an activity. We constantly try to raise productivities to ever increasing levels. Therefore, if a particular set of measures is used in its calculation - or even in a mental, nonquantitative "guesstimate" of productivity - there follows an endeavor to maximize what we perceive as output and to minimize what we consider as input. Should we be wrong in our choice of what constitutes outputs and what deserves to be used as inputs, we would be on a track of maximizing fictitious, valueless or dangerous parameters in what we call "productivity." This may well result in long-term hazards and harm to the enterprise. In R&D activities we have only rudimentary assessments of quantitative measures of outputs or inputs and less knowledge of the mechanisms which convert inputs into outputs. Hence, a too-early adoption of a productivity parameter for R&D activities may harden into short-term apparent benefits and long-term decay or misdirection. Roberta Miller highlighted this danger, I believe, wisely.

A third danger exists in what might be called the "search under the lamp syndrome." Just like the young boy who searched for his lost dime in the area lit by the street lamp, even though he had dropped it twenty feet away where it was dark, we might emphasize quantifiable, measurable factors - just because we can measure them - in preference to the more difficult to measure qualitative factors which may be, in fact, more significant. One obvious example is that we can measure increases in the short-term profitability of our equipment or processes resulting from trouble-shooting applied research more readily and accurately than we can evaluate the eventual impact of a breakthrough in physics, chemistry, or the life sciences. Thus "productivity," as measured by the output of incremental profits per unit input of dollars per annum (or of man-years of effort), will be more readily demonstrable to the powers-in-charge of policy and the purse strings than will any speculative "guesstimates" of the future benefits from breakthrough achievements. Such short-term figures (published quarterly or annually) could have an inhibiting effect on the undertaking of high risk, but more profound, research and development involving novel ideas and creative concept of truly great value. It is better to wait for further knowledge before we set standards of achievement in the form of productivity measures. "Productivity" is, at present, an inappropriate term to apply to R&D activities.

My second conclusion is that the subject is of obvious importance and deserves a great deal of further study. Thus, if we willingly abandon the use of the word "productivity," we must not thereby abandon the subject. How then shall we study it? I believe we should adopt a concept other than "productivity."

INDICATORS, NOT MEASURES

I would have preferred to recommend that we establish a program of study into "R&D Values." But the word and concept of "value" is perhaps as unnecessarily vague at this time as "productivity" is too technical and precise. So I recommend instead, in line with Charles Falk and Roberta Miller, that we concentrate a program on the study of Indicators of Industrial R&D. We would be in the good company of serious students of other difficult-to-define and more difficult-to-evaluate human activities. Students of trends in innovation, or of trends in the national economy, find "indicators" useful parameters.

The very use of the plural in "indicators" is a clear warning that none of them is necessarily an exclusive or an exhaustive measure of what we seek. Each taken separately and all of them together are simply pointers, not necessarily implying rigorous logical necessity between what they measure or describe and the effectiveness of the R&D activity; each of them may indicate or point to a different aspect of the R&D enterprise. Thus, we shall be prepared, because of our previous experience with other indicators, for our indicators sometimes to point to short-term and other times to long-term trends, and on occasion even to point in opposite directions. We shall then be in a more cautious mood when we attempt to draw sweeping conclusions affecting major strategies and policies before we have learnt what really makes our R&D enterprise work.

Indicators would consider both the input and the output side of R&D. Indeed, an output indicator for research may be an input indicator for future development, just as the whole set of R&D output indicators may serve as a single input indicator for innovation. When the indicators are numerable or measurable, we will also have the privilege and advantage of the ability to manipulate them mathematically to yield more complex (and perhaps more powerful) indicators of the costs and benefits of industrial R&D, without setting too rigid a limitation on our thinking.

Indicators would have the further advantage of selectivity, allowing us to evaluate R&D activities in different sectors - government, academia, institutions, and industry - or different types of research activities - basic, applied, or development - or different scales or units of organization - individual industrial laboratory, a corporation's total activity, a particular industry, or the whole national endeavor.

My third conclusion is that we are in urgent need of identifying as many indicators of industrial R&D activity as possible and of studying them in depth in order to formulate some reasonably cohesive concepts of the primary factors that enhance or reduce the possibilities of success in our industrial R&D enterprises.

I would suggest we start by collecting factual data on currently used indicators of science, but apply them to industrial R&D activities. For input indicators, we might examine absolute dollar expenditures; expenditure as fractions of sales or of profit or of capital investment or of dividends; number of professionals involved in R&D, broken down by field of science and level of education; and those numbers as ratios of total personnel in the corporation, or the particular industry, or per 1,000 employees. For output indicators, we may cite number of papers published in reviewed journals or other bibliometric data; citation indices; citation by foreign countries; number of patents issued; number of new products exceeding a given figure for sales or income values introduced per unit of time; profits from new products, processes or services per unit of time; and number of honors received by the unit's researchers.

These are well-known indicators already in use, but we should also search for newer indicators. Drawing on information theory, Art Damask has proposed in his paper what we might call a "surprise index": the more unexpected the result of a research activity, the greater its novelty and, possibly, its usefulness or its value as a new item of knowledge. We could also develop indicators of a more qualitative nature, such as peer ranking of a laboratory or research institution. One study of 30 chemical companies correlated price-earnings (P/E) ratios with the ratios of research expenditures per dollar of sales; and a significant linear relationship was found. [J.J. Gilman, "Stock Price and Optimum Research Spending," Research Management Review, January 1978, pp. 34-36.] Similar studies on other industries or companies may provide a new indicator. Social or environmental impacts traceable to R&D may provide positive - or negative - indicators. The number of laboratory alumni in positions of seniority in a corporation, industry, or the nation could provide another output indicator. Government contracts earned because of the company's achievement or reputation in R&D could provide yet another indicator. Even the number of invited interactions with other research organizations, in academic seminars, or in national and international conferences could provide an indicator of how a researcher or an organization is ranked or viewed by other professionals.

NO PRECONCEPTIONS

Thus, indicators provide richly varied points of view from which to observe and evaluate an R&D activity or organization. At this stage of our knowledge, data gathering with the minimum of preconceptions of what constitute significant measures or rankings appears to be the prime necessity. I would recommend that a very wide variety of indicators be systematically documented for many years and for as many research and development organizations as is feasible and practicable.

Only after a great many sets of such data and indicators are gathered for United States and foreign research enterprises - for different sectors (national, government, industrial, academic and nonprofit as well as for-profit research institutes) of different sizes, and serving different industries - should a systematic study be made of correlational and causal relationships among the indicators. It may then be possible, I believe, to uncover significant factors that enhance or hinder the success of research and development efforts.

Afterword

Concluding Comments on R&D Productivity: Where Do We Stand?

Herbert I. Fusfeld

The views presented in this volume combine to give a sense of the complexity of issues which R&D productivity presents us, and of the many different starting points from which to approach the subject. This very diversity, while intended to demonstrate the breadth of the subject, may indeed produce an initial aura of confusion. Someone considering R&D productivity on the basis of these chapters alone might find it difficult to define a clear path to both understanding and improvement.

Part of the reason for this is that the chapters took a long-range stance, seeking theoretical understanding and improvement. Let me instead return to the pragmatic. Our short-term intent was a look at the subject (more or less simultaneously) by both practitioners and theoreticians. Both now have a sense of the forest as well as of their individual trees. Presumably, their future comments and studies will reflect this. That is a step forward.

Logically, understanding should come before improvement, and it is hard to claim that a description of a subject tells us much about correlations. The overall summary perspective, so ably presented by Alfred Nissan, focuses on fundamentals. He reminds us that we must start with definitions of quantities that can be measured, and then measure them. And until we can do this, even the use of the phrase "R&D productivity" bestows a quantitative characteristic on the subject to an extent that is not yet deserved and is possibly misleading.

So back to pragmatism. Can we proceed to seek improvements before we have a full understanding? Of course. We do so everyday in many fields. Better to seek change cautiously, with the full knowledge that understanding escapes us, than be guided into action by the illusion of understanding or be locked into inaction by the awareness of our ignorance. I believe our discussions in these chapters permit the practitioners to proceed on the basis of broader horizons, while theorists can strengthen their models and move closer to actual working systems.

The phrase "R&D productivity" has quite properly attracted attention. Obviously, the concept of getting more value from an activity that accounts for close to $70 billion of effort in the United States alone, and which influences wide economic and social objectives, should indeed attract attention.

Yet there is concern that "productivity" is not a proper concept for R&D; that it borrows unfairly from a well-established economic concept, thus implying substance where there is only abstraction; and that some more descriptive phrase be used to emphasize the qualitative and, indeed, subjective nature of the R&D process.

I propose that we do discuss "R&D productivity." There are quantities to observe; we will strengthen the understanding of both R&D and economics by simultaneous attention to the realities of R&D productivity and the ambiguities of economic productivity; and the attention attracted will reduce much of the vagueness and confusion that exists.

One theme emerging from the chapters is that there is a breadth and richness in the R&D enterprise that calls for careful definition of the particular package or component of the R&D system under discussion. General "R&D productivity" may indeed be too vague for coherent discussion. But the R&D productivity of a laboratory, company, or an industry can be described in specific terms - though not, of course, the same terms in each case.

Thus, Bruce Merrifield discussed the importance of industrial research in the need for capital investment. Richard Levin described the impact of R&D investment on the technical progress of the semiconductor industry. And Arthur Damask presented an ingenious concept for a mathematical approach to classifying and analyzing the quality of output from a broad based research laboratory.

The common-sense notion of productivity in any effort is that there is some output deriving from a set of inputs. These factors are present in the conduct of R&D, but with a uniqueness that should be made explicit. The inputs are describable in the same terms as almost all activities within our society - namely, the number and kinds of personnel and the accompanying financial investment. However, except for the area of basic research, the direct output from an R&D laboratory is rarely what the sponsor wants or can measure. For R&D produces knowledge, and this is a means to an end, whether the sponsor is private or public, a single corporation, or society as a whole. Even basic research is not exempt from this judgment intellectually, although the time for conversion to other ends is so long that we must treat it as a separate entity in practice.

The outputs for which we invest in R&D are therefore indirect, and result from conversion of the direct output of knowledge to the form of added value which we want and can measure. This adds two more elements to the concept of R&D productivity. First, we must define our system to include some economic or social structure beyond the R&D organization alone. The problems and intricacies of studying R&D productivity in the context of a social indicator were ably examined in the chapters by Roberta Miller and Charles Falk. Second, there are inputs for this broader system, for the process of converting knowledge, that must be considered in a true accounting of R&D productivity. This is evident in much of Lowell Steele's chapter.

These issues are illustrative of two separate but related themes that weave in and out of the book. Depending on the particular author's approach, he or she is talking either about the effectiveness with which a particular R&D activity is conducted or about the economic value derived from that activity. This dual perspective is obviously a principal cause of the uncertainty at the root of the subject. Let me offer an example.

The increasing use and value of robotics in our industrial processes can be enhanced considerably by development of "vision" for robots. This presumably requires a major systems effort incorporating optics, electronics, mechanics, and so on. Suppose that a successful effort would result in added market value of $2 billion for the suppliers, and considerably more value to society from the use of such facilities in production. Now, assume that a technical organization can carry out the necessary development for $100 million in five years. Clearly, there is a very great economic value to such a program however we choose to measure the results of the R&D activity.

But, we can also assume that several technical organizations addressing the same problem might reach a successful conclusion in the same time for different costs of, say, $60 million to $150 million. Or that the program would be completed at different intervals of time from, say, four years to eight years. We are now talking about the effectiveness with which R&D is conducted. For much of our consideration, "R&D productivity" refers more to the second characteristic than the first, but the complete picture includes both.

I did not intend to drift into further details, since I have no added facts beyond the concepts described in these chapters. My purpose was simply to emphasize that there is a valid common-sense meaning to the notion of "R&D productivity," but each application requires careful definition of the system and the outputs. Conversely, the apparent vagueness of the broad concept when a specific system is not so defined must not discourage us from considering the concept, but should remind us that we should not consider R&D productivity without a well-defined system.

The broad framework sketched in this book should help in the identification and stimulation of research programs. Questions have been raised that call for contributions in economics, management, sociology, and mathematics. Long-term improvements will result only when such studies can refer to a common structure, and this requires a basis for discussion among all these interests. I believe the organization of these chapters through the mechanism of a seminar series has been a constructive step in this direction.

Selected Bibliography of R&D Productivity

Farook Chowdhury

A. ECONOMIC EFFECTS OF R&D

1. Abramowitz, Moses. 1956. "Resource and Output Trends in the U.S. Since 1870," American Economic Review XLVI, no. 2.

2. Agnew, C. and D. Wise. 1980. "The Impact of Research and Development on Productivity," research supported by National Science Foundation, Grant PRA-7722611.

3. Bryan, Glenn C. 1973. "The Role of Basic Research in the Total R&D Process," Research Management XVI, no. 1.

4. Fabricant, Solomon. 1954. "Economic Progress and Economic Change," 34th Annual Report of the National Bureau of Economic Research, New York.

5. Fernelius, W.C. and W.H. Waldo. 1980. "Role of Basic Research in Industrial Innovation," Research Management XXIII, no. 4.

6. Freeman, C. 1969. "Measurement of Output of Research and Experimental Development: A Review Paper," UNESCO.

7. Griliches, Zvi. 1958. "Research Cost and Social Returns: Hybrid Corn and Related Innovation," Journal of Political Economy LXVI, no. 5.

8. Griliches, Zvi. 1964. "Research Expenditures, Education and the Aggregate Agricultural Production Function," American Economic Review LIV, no. 6.

9. Griliches, Zvi. 1973. "Research Expenditures and Growth Accounting," in B.R. Williams, ed., Science and Technology in Economic Growth, London: Macmillan.

10. Griliches, Zvi. 1979. "Issues in Assessing the Contribution of Research and Development to Productivity Growth," Bell Journal of Economics 10, no. 1.

11. Griliches, Zvi. 1964. "Research Expenditures, Education and the Aggregate Agricultural Production Function," American Economic Review LIV, no. 6.

12. Hill, C. and J. Utterback, eds. 1979. Technological Innovation for a Dynamic Economy, New York: Pergamon Press.

13. Klein, B. 1977. Dynamic Economics, Cambridge: Harvard University Press.

14. Mansfield, E. 1965. "Rates of Return from Industrial Research and Development," American Economic Review LV, no. 2.

15. Mansfield, E. 1968. Industrial Research and Technological Innovation, New York: Norton.

16. Mansfield, E. 1980. "Basic Research and Productivity Increase in Manufacturing," American Economic Review 70, no. 5.

17. Mansfield, E., J. Rapaport, A. Romeo, S. Wagner and G. Beardsley. 1977. "Social and Private Rates of Return from Industrial Innovation," Quarterly Journal of Economics XCI, no. 2.

18. Mansfield, E., J. Rapaport, J. Schnee, S. Wagner and M. Hamburger. 1971. Research and Innovation in the Modern Corporation, New York: W.W. Norton & Co.

19. Minasian, Jora. 1969. "Research and Development, Production Function and Rates of Return," American Economic Review LIX, no. 2.

20. Nadiri, M. Ishaq. 1970. "Some Approaches to the Theory and Measurement of Total Factor Productivity: A Survey," Journal of Economic Literature VIII, no. 4.

21. Nelson, R.R. and S.G. Winter. 1977. "Toward a Useful Theory of Innovation," Research Policy 6: 36.

22. Nelson, R.R., M.J. Peck and E.D. Kalachek. 1967. Technology, Economic Growth and Public Policy, Washington, D.C.: The Brookings Institution.

23. Pakes, A. and M. Schankerman. 1978. "The Rate of Obsolescence of Knowledge, Research Gestation Lags and the Private Rate of Return to Research Resources,"

Harvard Institute of Economic Research, Discussion Paper 659.

24. Peterson, Willis L. 1967. "Return to Poultry Research in the U.S.," Journal of Farm Economics 49, no. 3.

25. Quinn, James Brian. 1960. "How to Evaluate Research Output," Harvard Business Review 38, no. 2.

26. R&D and Economic Growth: Productivity, Papers and Proceedings of a Colloquium, 1971. National Science Foundation (NSF 72-303).

27. Scherer, F.M. 1965. "Firm Size, Market Structure, Opportunity, and the Output of Patented Inventories," American Economic Review LV, no. 5.

28. Scherer, F.M. and W.S. Comanor. 1969. "Patent Statistics as a Measure of Technical Change," Journal of Political Economy 77.

29. Schmookler, J. 1966. Investing and Economic Growth, Cambridge, Mass.: Harvard University Press.

30. Solow, Robert. 1957. "Technical Change and the Aggregate Production Function," Review of Economics and Statistics XXXIX, no. 3.

31. Terleckyj, N. 1970. "Effects of R&D on the Productivity Growth of Industries: An Exploratory Study," Washington, D.C.: National Planning Association.

32. Terleckyj, N. 1959. "Sources of Productivity Change." Unpublished Ph.D. thesis, New York: Columbia University.

33. Williams, B.R. 1973. Science and Technology in Economic Growth, London: Macmillan.

34. Science Indicators 1978. 1979. Report of the National Science Board.

B. MANAGERIAL ANALYSIS OF R&D

35. Aiken, Michael and Hage, Jerald. 1979. "The Organic Organization and Innovation," Sociology 5, no. 1.

36. Anderson, Arthur G. 1971. "Maintaining Vitality in R&D Organization," Research Management XIV, no. 4.

37. Badawy, M.K. 1976. "Applying Management by Objectives to R&D Labs," Research Management XIX, no. 6.

38.   Baker, N. and J. Freeland. 1975. "Recent advances in R&D Benefit Measurement and Project Selection Methods," Management Sciences 21, no. 10.

39.   Baker, N. and Pound, W.H. 1964. "R&D Project Selection: Where We Stand," IEEE Transaction on Engineering Management EM-11.

40.   Balthasar, H.U., A.A.R. Boschi and M.M. Menke. 1978. "Calling the Shots in R&D," Harvard Business Review 56, no. 3.

41.   Baxter, H.G. and H.D. Grabowski. 1973. "Rivalry in Industrial R&D: An Empirical Study," Journal of Industrial Economics XXI, no. 3.

42.   Berman, S.I. 1973. "Integrating the R&D Department into the Business Team," Research Management XVI, no. 4.

43.   Beattie, C.J. and R.D. Reader. 1971. Quantitative Management in R&D, London: Chapman Hall Ltd.

44.   Bissell, Herbert D. 1971. "Research and Marketing - Rivals or Partners?" Research Management XIV, no. 3.

45.   Bobis, A.H. et al. 1971. "A Funds Allocation Method to Improve the Odds for Research Successes," Research Management XIV, no. 2.

46.   Boschi, A.A.R., H.U. Balthasar and M.M. Menke. 1979. "Quantifying and Forecasting Exploratory Research Success," Research Management XXII, no. 5.

47.   Brown, Rex V. 1969. Research and Credibility of Estimates: An Appraisal Tool for Executives and Researchers, Harvard University Press.

48.   Bucher, George C. and Richard C. Gray. 1971. "The Principles of Motivation and How to Apply Them" Research Management XIV, no. 3.

49.   Bulat, T.J. 1979. "Ways to better Liaison Between Corporate Research and Operations," Research Management XXII, no. 1.

50.   Butler, O.B. 1976. "What Marketing Expects from R&D," Research Management XIX, no. 1.

51.   Carlsson, B., P. Keane and J.B. Martin. 1976. "R&D Organization as Learning Systems," Sloan Management Review 17, no. 3.

52.   Chan, James L. 1978. "Organizational Concensus Regarding the Relative Importance of Research Output Indicators," Accounting Review LIII, no. 2.

53. Clark, Paul. 1977. "A Profitability Project Selection Method," Research Management XX, no. 6.

54. Clayton, Ross. 1971. "A Convergent Approach to R&D Planning and Project Selection," Research Management XIV, no. 5.

55. Cooper, M.J. 1978. "An Evaluation System for Project Selection," Research Management XXI, no. 4.

56. Diehl, Peter and J.R. Howell. 1976. "Improving Communication with the R&D Team" Research Management XIX, no. 1.

57. Faust, Richard E. 1971. "Project Selection in the Pharmaceutical Industry," Research Management XIV, no. 5.

58. Foster, Richard N. 1971. "Estimating Research Payoff by Internal Rate of Return Method," Research Management XIV, no. 6.

59. Gambino, Anthony, and Morris Gartenberg. 1979. "Costing and Reporting R&D Operations," Research Management XXII, no. 4.

60. Gee, Robert E. 1971. "Current Project Selection Practices," Research Management XIV, no. 5.

61. Gomersall, Earl R. 1971. "Current and Future Factors Affecting the Motivation of Scientists, Engineers and Technicians," Research Management XIV, no. 3.

62. Gruber, W.H., O.H. Poensgen and F. Prakke. 1973. "The Isolation of R&D from Corporation Management," Research Management XVI, no. 6.

63. Helin, A.F. and W.E. Souder. 1974. "Experimental Test of a Q-Sort Procedure for Prioritizing R&D Projects," IEEE Transactions on Engineering Management EM-21, no. 4.

64. Hertz, D.B. 1964. "Risk Analysis in Capital Investment," Harvard Business Review 42, no. 1.

65. Landis, Fred. 1971. "What Makes Technical Men Happy and Productive," Research Management XIV, no. 3.

66. Lindsay, Edwin M. 1971. "Financial Management of R&D: Planning and Budgeting, Project Authorization and Financial Reporting," Research Management XIV, no. 4.

67. Litterer, J.A. 1970. "Research Department Within Large Organization," California Management Review XII, no. 3.

68. Lockett, Geoffrey A. and Anthony E. Gear. 1972. "Programme Selection in Research and Development," Management Science 18, no. 10.

69. Mansfield, E. 1963. "Size of Firm, Market Structure and Innovation," Journal of Political Economy LXXI, no. 6.

70. Mansfield, E. and S. Wagner. 1975. "Organizational and Strategic Factors Associated with Probabilities of Success in Industrial R&D," Journal of Business 48, no. 2.

71. Mechlin, George F. and Daniel Berg. 1980. "Evaluating Research - ROI is Not Enough," Harvard Business Review 58, no. 5.

72. Merrifield, D. Bruce. 1979. "Nurturing the Innovator," Research Management XXII, no. 6.

73. Monte Leone, J.P. 1976. "How R&D and Marketing Can Work Together," Research Management XIX, no. 2.

74. Moore, D.C. and D.S. Davies. 1977. "The Dual Ladder: Establishing and Operating It," Research Management XX, no. 4.

75. Moore, J.R. and N.R. Baker. 1969. "Computational Analysis of Scoring Models for R&D Project Selection," Management Science 16, no. 6.

76. Paolillo, Joseph G. and Warren B. Brown. 1978. "How Organizational Factors Affect Innovation," Research Management XXI, no. 2.

77. Roberts, Edward B. 1979. "Organizational Approaches," Research Management XXII, no. 6.

78. Rubenstein, A.H., A.K. Chakrasarti, R.D. O'Keefe, W.E. Souder and H.C. Young. 1976. "Factors Influencing Innovation Success at the Project Level," Research Management XIX, no. 3.

79. Souder, William E. 1978. "A System for Using R&D Project Evaluation Methods," Research Management XXI, no. 5.

80. Souder, William E. 1972. "A Scoring Methodology for Assessing the Suitability of Management Science Models," Management Science 18, no. 10.

81. Souder, William E. 1975. "Field Studies With a Q-Sort/Nominal Group Process for Selecting R&D Projects," Research Policy 4.

82. Stahl, Michael J. and Joseph A. Steger. 1977. "Measuring Innovation and Productivity - A Peer Rating Approach," Research Management XX, no. 1.

83. Villiers, Raymond. 1964. R&D: Planning and Control, a research study prepared for the Financial Executives Research Foundation, New York.

84. Whaley, Wilson M. and R.A. Williams. 1971. "A Profit-
     Oriented Approach to Project Selection," Research Man-
     agement XIV, no. 5.

85. Whitman, Eric S. and Edward F. Landau. 1971. "Project
     Selection in the Chemical Industry," Research Management
     XIV, no. 5.

86. Hughes Aircraft Corporation. 1978. R&D Productivity,
     Culver City, California, Second Edition.

Index

143

List of Seminar Series Participants

1. William Abernathy
   Harvard Business School

2. Stephen F. Adler
   Stauffer Chemical Co.

3. Arthur Anderson
   International Business
   Machines Corp.

4. Alden S. Bean
   National Science Foundation

5. Alfred E. Brown
   Celanese Corp.

6. J. Hoyt Chaloud
   Proctor & Gamble

7. F.R. Charvat
   Union Carbide

8. Donald W. Collier
   Borg Warner Corp.

9. Charles V. Cosgrove
   Merck & Co., Inc.

10. Lee L. Davenport
    GTE

11. Faye Duchin
    Institute for Economic
       Analysis,
    New York University

12. John M. Dutton
    Graduate School of
       Business Administra-
       tion,
    New York University

13. Charles E. Falk
    National Science
       Foundation

14. Steward Flaschen
    ITT

15. Denos Gazis
    IBM

16. J.E. Goldman
    Xerox Corp.

17. N. Bruce Hannay
    Bell Laboratories

18. William M. Holliday
    Consultant

19. Donald D. King
North American Philips

20. Harold G. Kaufman
Polytechnic Institute
of NY

21. Charles F. Larson
Industrial Research
Institute

22. Richard Levin
Yale University

23. Wassily Leontief
Institute for Economic
Analysis,
New York University

24. Igor Makarov
The USSR Embassy

25. Donald G. Manly
Anaconda Industries

26. D. Bruce Merrifield
The Continental Group

27. Roberta Balstad Miller
Social Science Research
Council

28. Mary Mogee
U.S. Department
of Commerce

29. M. Ishaq Nadiri
Department of Economics,
New York University

30. John H. Nininger
General Electric Co.

31. Alfred H. Nissan
Westvaco Corp.

32. John B. Northrop
Standard and Poors

33. H.J. Novy
Novy, Eddison & Partners

34. Eli M. Pearce
Polytechnic Institute
of New York

35. David Z. Robinson
Carnegie Corp. of
New York

36. Brian Rushton
Celanese Corp.

37. Devandra Sahal
Graduate School of
Business Administra-
tion,
New York University

38. Mark Schankerman
Department of Economics,
New York University

39. A. George Schillinger
Polytechnic Institute
of New York

40. Frederick Seitz
The Rockefeller
University

41. Jacob Schwartz
Courant Institute,
New York University

42. Lowell W. Steele
General Electric Co.

43. Klaus-Heinrich Standke
UNESCO/Paris

44. Lawrence E. Swable, Jr.
Exxon Research &
Eng. Co.

45. Annie Thomas
Graduate School of
Business Administra-
tion,
New York University

46. Michael Tyler
    Graduate School of Public
    Administration,
    New York University

47. David A. Vermilyea
    General Electric Co.

48. Paul Wachtel
    Graduate School of
    Business Administration,
    New York University

49. N. Richard Werthaner
    Exxon Corp.

50. Guenther Wilhelon
    Exxon Research &
    Eng. Co.

51. Francis W. Wolek
    U.S. Department of
    Commerce

CENTER FOR SCIENCE & TECHNOLOGY POLICY

1. Herbert I. Fusfeld
   Director

2. Richard R. Nelson
   Consultant

3. Carmela S. Haklisch
   Assistant Director

4. Hedvah L. Shuchman
   Consultant

5. Lois S. Peters
   Research Associate

6. Richard N. Langlois
   Research Associate

7. Arthur C. Damask
   Visiting Professor

8. Nico Hazewindus
   Visiting Fellow

9. Mary N. Damask
   Consultant

10. Farook Chowdhury
    Research Assistant

11. John D. Tooker
    Research Assistant

About the Editors and Contributors

HERBERT I. FUSFELD is director of the Center for Science and Technology Policy, Graduate School of Business Administration, New York University. He has held the positions of director of research for the American Machine and Foundry Corporation and director of research for Kennecott Copper Corporation. Professional and government activities have included membership on the U.S.-USSR Joint Commission for Scientific and Technical Cooperation, the Advisory Committee on Transnational Enterprises, U.S. Department of State, and the Advisory Group on Technology and Economic Growth at OECD. Dr. Fusfeld is a former president of the Industrial Research Institute and is on the Advisory Council, National Science Foundation.

RICHARD N. LANGLOIS, a research assistant professor at the Center, has been involved in the Center's recent project on the effectiveness of government-sponsored R&D in the civilian sector. Dr. Langlois is also on the faculty of New York University's Department of Economics. His research interests include the economics of innovation and the role of information and knowledge in economic theory.

WILLIAM J. ABERNATHY is a Professor at the Graduate School of Business Administration, Harvard University.

ARTHUR G. ANDERSON is an IBM Vice President and President of IBM's General Products Division.

ARTHUR C. DAMASK is Visiting Professor at the Center for Science and Technology Policy, New York University, and Professor of Physics at Queens College of the City University of New York.

CHARLES E. FALK is director of the Division of Science Resource Studies of the National Science Foundation.

RICHARD C. LEVIN is Professor of Economics and Professor of Organization and Management at Yale University.

D. BRUCE MERRIFIELD is Vice President, Technology and Venture Management, the Continental Group, Inc.

ROBERTA BALSTAD MILLER is Executive Director of the Consortium of Social Science Organizations, Washington, D.C.

RICHARD R. NELSON is Professor of Economics and Director of the Institution for Social and Policy Studies at Yale University.

ALFRED H. NISSAN, Visiting Professor at the Center for Science and Technology Policy, New York University, recently retired as vice president and corporate research director of the Westvaco Corporation.

LOWELL STEELE is Staff Executive-Corporate Technology Planning for the General Electric Company.